TRAVELS WITH PENNY:
TRUE TRAVEL TALES OF A GAY GUY
AND HIS MOM

David Alan Morrison

TRAVELS WITH PENNY:
TRUE TRAVEL TALES OF A GAY GUY AND HIS MOM

ACKNOWLEDGEMENTS:

There's a special place in my heart for those people in my life who have never wavered in their support and encouragement. I thank them all. But this project has some special "Thanks": the Iowa Writer's Workshop "Memoir" class during the summer of 2008 for prodding me to write this memoir; Brian "London" Ellis for his computer genius; Holly for her laughs; Keith A. Gehrig for his honesty, and, of course, Mom.

PART ONE
1998: New York

Two things flashed through my mind when I opened the door to the sex shop to find my mother standing in front of the display case talking to a tall salesman wearing a leather harness, jock strap and a dog collar. The first was, "Oh, crap!" The second was, "I hate it when Dad's right."

Watching my mother investigate the testicle torture devices, cock rings and nipple clamps was not even close to being on the weekend's itinerary. It was so far removed from my itinerary, it was in a separate zip code. This New York trip was supposed to be a celebration of my thirty-fifth birthday; it was supposed to be an opportunity for me to have one last grand hurrah before the fall semester kicked in and buried me under the pressure of literature reviews, critical analysis papers and thesis research. I envisioned this weekend to be a fun-filled romp around the Big Apple, not a safari through Leather Wonderland with my mother.

Life: it's what happens while you're busy making other plans. Or, as my mom would say, "Tough toenails, Tony!" which she usually follows up with, "Life sucks! Then you die!" Is there any wonder why therapists drool when I walk into a room?

The previous February, I excavated my apartment looking for those things that I considered precious, so I could lovingly gather them up and take them on my journey to that esteemed promised land: GRADUATE SCHOOL. I should have realized my life was in for some form of cosmic shake up when all my worldly possessions in my two-bedroom apartment dwindled down into a couple boxes and a shopping bag. I threw the stuff and my annoying loud cat into my Dihatsu Rocky and turned my back on Seattle. I faced my tomorrows with all the bushy-eyed naivety of a five-year-old at Christmas; eager to begin my Master's program at the University of Kentucky. The idealistic awe of my future toppled off the pedestal upon entering the Bluegrass State and crossing over into the twilight zone.

I exited the expressway when I saw a sign for Versailles, although I couldn't decipher my handwriting well enough to read which exit I was to take. Since I had no idea if this was the correct exit or not, I crossed my fingers and kept driving. After a few miles of nothing, scenes from *Children of the Corn* began playing through my mind. I began to fear that I'd be found dead in my car with a couple boxes of useless crap and a starving cat, so I betrayed my gender and pulled into a gas station to ask directions. I admit it: I panicked. Sue me.

"Is this the way to Versailles?" I asked the pimply-faced young woman with greasy hair and stained smock. I pronounced the town VER-SIGH, after the town in France of the same name, which--let's face it--seemed logical.

She looked at me blankly. "Wha?" she asked. The people in Kentucky tend to delete the final consonants on words, making them sound like they carry pebbles in their mouths.

"Ver-sigh," I said. "I'm lost. Is it this way?"

"I ain't never hear o' that place."

"It's supposed to be around here somewhere," I said, showing her the address of the bed and breakfast.

She took the paper, read it and her eyes lit up. "Oh! You mean Ver Sales!" she exclaimed. "Go on dow that road a piece. It right there," she said pointing the direction.

Welcome to Kentucky, where they honor famous cities by naming towns after them, then purposely butchering the pronunciation. A week or so later, the UK wildcats won the Final Four basketball championships and practically destroyed Lexington in celebratory glee. I didn't even know what "Final Four" meant--I don't follow sports. I assumed the radio announcer butchered "Fab Five" and the rowdiness was about a reinvention of the Fab Four.

I mention this because when Mom came face-to-face with our dog-collared friend, we happened to be in Greenwich Village, the birthplace of Gay Liberation where I am currently touring along with my 54-year-old mother and two friends of mine, Troy and Gary, who are (you guessed it) from Ver Sales. How Troy and Gary got involved in this birthday trip is easy to explain: they were travel agents with a taste for chaos. Their birthday gift to me was to arrange this short holiday in New York as a tribute to arriving at thirty-five while clinging to more than a handful of hair. How my mother came to join us is not so easy to explain, as it just . . . happened. It's modus operandi when Mom and I are together, things just . . . happen.

However this trip was our maiden voyage traveling together. Previously, traveling with either of my parents happened vicariously. Namely, they did the traveling and I listened to their stories with envy in my heart that they had the money to seek adventure while I squandered every buck I ever made. After they returned from a month-long visit to see my sister, Mom and I sat at the kitchen table, armed with a pot of coffee and pastries to look at her Italian acquisitions. I was eager to hear about their first trip out of the United States, as Dad liked to frequent places where he felt comfortable--namely any land mass flying the American flag and sheltering a good plate of biscuits and gravy. He enjoyed cruising the open roads of rural America because it meant that he could stay in hotels that advertised on Super Bowl Sunday, or RV parks large enough to accommodate their 40-foot-long rolling Taj Mahal. He liked exotic food, as long as it came with a chocolate milkshake with a tiny, paper American Flag sticking out of the whipped cream. Mom, on the other hand, wanted to take the road less traveled or, in this case, a road frequently traveled by everyone else except her. She handed me several picture post cards and I flipped through them.

"You're giving them to me?" I asked. "Why didn't you mail them?"

"Hell! We'd be back before you got them! This way, I save the cost of postage."

That's my mom. Never pass up an opportunity to pinch a penny. "Why did you come home early?"

"Your dad was freaking out."

"Freaking out?" I asked. "Freaking out" is one of those expressions that you hope never to hear come out of your parent's mouth. There's a youthfulness about that term that makes it seem that anyone over the age of 50 should be allergic to it.

She shook her head. "I don't know, David, he just became so . . . anxious." I waited for her to continue. It was a long pause, but not one of those where you wonder if she knew the answer. It was the pause of someone who didn't want to confess knowing the answer.

"He got so frustrated at not being able to speak the language, confused over the currency exchange . . ."

"Why didn't you just charge it?" I suggested. "The credit card company does all the rate exchange for you."

She shrugged. "We did. But it was more than that . . . he didn't know his way around . . . it bothered him that he couldn't read the street signs . . . he felt like he had no control over anything. He just flipped out. He came to me in Italy and told he wanted to go home."

"You agreed?" I asked, obsessing about where the hell she picked up the expression, "flipped out".

She nodded. "I was having a great time, too. I loved Europe. All the churches, the history . . . I find it fascinating."

"I want to go to Europe sometime," I said. "I like going to a place and just . . . wandering. No plans. No schedules. Just . . . being in a different place."

"Me, too."

I looked at her, looking at the photos. What would it be like for her not to go back to Europe again? Knowing that she's only scratched the surface of the centuries-old continent, but would never return to explore it further? We sat for a moment, she fidgeting over something on the table and I wondering what it must be like to have an explorer's heart, married to someone with the heart of a farmer. Before I knew what I was saying--and surprising myself--I blurted out, "You know, we should travel together sometime."

"That would be great!" She smiled. "I think we would travel well together." Her eyes lit up. I could travel with my mom. Seriously-- how hard could it be?

Fast forward to a short decade later when Troy and Gary pulled some strings to get the New York hotels and round-trip airfare at a hell of a discount. They told me the rates were based upon double-occupancy and suggested I bring someone with me. I suspect they assumed I would invite one of their eligible single friends in the hopes I was desperate enough to grab the first single guy that came along and stop mourning the evaporation of my latest relationship. I have no idea what went through their minds when I said I'd invite my mother along, although I think Gary choked on a granola bar.

The plan was simple: Troy and Gary and I would meet mom at JFK and the four of us would take a cab to Manhattan. Troy and Gary would share one of the rooms of the rented apartment while Mom and I took the second. Each couple would operate independently, relax and enjoy the long weekend. Mom agreed to the ground rules, as did Troy and Gary. It was Dad who balked.

"You're going to get her killed in some gang war or drive-by shooting," he snapped at me from his La-Z-Boy when I visited Tennessee to propose the trip to Mom.

"Are we going to go to the theatre?" Mom yelled from the bedroom, obviously eavesdropping. She was mentally packing weeks before we left. Mom's nothing if not thorough.

"Dad, nobody is going to die in a drive-by shooting," I assured him.

Dad glared at me and muttered under his breath, "I think it's great you two go someplace together. But if you're going to spend money, go someplace I won't take her, like Europe."

"Maybe next time."

He shook his head and yelled at the defensive linebacker on TV. "I'm worried."

"We'll call you every day. How does that sound?"

"I'm worried about New York. No telling what trouble you two will get into there."

"I do not get into trouble," I protested. Then, as an afterthought, "Not anymore."

He grumbled and cracked open another peanut. "This is a bad idea."

"I want to do something special for my birthday, Dad. Go somewhere I've never been."

"Branson, Missouri, has some great concerts. I'll go with you to Branson."

"I don't want to travel some tourist trap, Dad," I pleaded. "I want to do something memorable . . . fun . . . interesting."

"Dollywood's interesting."

"Dad, why don't you come with us?"

He shook his head and flipped through the channels. He hated commercials. "I ain't going to New York! Dirty, big, noisy, crazy people . . . they can keep it for all I care." He looked at me and popped another peanut into his mouth. "Don't take her to any of those shady, New York, low-life places, like gay bars."

"Relax, Dad," I laughed. "A gay bar is probably the safest place for her to be."

He looked me dead in the eye and said, "She's your responsibility. If anything happens to her, I'm blaming you."

"What's the worst that could happen, Pop?" I asked as he turned back to the game.

Note to self: Stop tempting fate.

RELATED TANGENT #1

Extract of my Journal dated Friday, August 3, 2007

My dad and I never went to a bar in my entire life; in fact, we barely drank. So why were we meeting in a bar? Here we sat like some textbook description of redneck kin in a dark bar, complete with old wooden floor, exposed ceiling beams and polished brass. The huge mirror behind the bar put the finishing touches on the cliché ridden scene. Except, of course, for the fact Dad was dead.

For a dead guy, he looked great--the dim light shone a dark illumination across the bar's surface, yet I could see him clearly. He wore a long-sleeved shirt that appeared to be flannel and held the beer bottle between the thumb and forefinger of his right hand. Despite the low light, every feature was visible, from the worry creases in his forehead to the crow's feet lines around his eyes. He wasn't happy per se; there wasn't a broad smile or odd laugh, yet he wasn't unhappy either. He looked like a man stuck in the cycle of remembrance, and everything appeared clear and sensible in the way only 20/20 hindsight can do.

"It's a path she has to walk through on her own," he sounded matter-of-fact and unemotional.

"She's going to be alone," I said.

"There's nothing you can do. This is a part of the path that only she can take." He took no pleasure in saying this. He sounded sad. I knew these words hurt him, but just like cleaning the bathroom, there are some things that just need to be done.

"It's going to be okay," he said, not looking at me. "She'll be okay."

I let myself cry. Ever since his death, I wanted to let go and even allowed myself to leak a bit around the eyes. Crying is an act I've always reserved for times of utmost privacy, best done alone in a remote location far away from human eyes--kind of like masturbation–but I couldn't stop myself. I cried and cried, unable to control myself. We hate each other, this impulse to cry and myself. It tries to overtake me and I battle it until it retreats into my psyche once more like a wounded animal. I don't feel emotions as much as I beat them into submission. My shrink thinks this is a fascinating character trait. He likes to talk about it endlessly. I don't like my therapist much, come to think of it.

But this time felt worse than any crying jag had ever felt: How can he say she would be okay? Ever since I heard the news of his death a sense of unbelievability had crept through me. We always know someday our parents will die, but when it actually happens, it remains in that state of suspended animation like some kind of bad dream that won't go away; I vacillated between uncontrolled shaking, unexplainable hyperventilation and utter panic. I expected the shock of his death, I knew I would feel a sense of loss, but hadn't expected the physical pain that accompanied it. My chest, arms and abdomen hurt like someone beat the shit out of me. I could barely breath without concentrating. After I arrived in Tennessee and spent time with my mother, I now felt afraid for her: How can she wake every morning and go along eating, cleaning, cooking, now that a man who she lived with for the past 47 years was gone? How can she sleep in a bed where, until this week, another human had slept at her side? How can she feed the cat knowing that this cat liked Dad better than her?

"There's nothing you can do."

I tried to respond, but nothing came out. Then Dad was gone and I woke up in the guest room, covered in sweat.

Ever since arriving in Tennessee for Dad's funeral, I'd been hoping and praying that I would have some kind of supernatural experience. I desperately wanted to be one of those people who saw my dead father and have him depart some other-worldly wisdom upon me. I wanted contact from the spirit world. I wanted an apparition to speak to me.

Instead, he appears in a dream and talks about my mother. When he was alive, he made everything about her and now that he's dead, he <u>still</u> makes everything about her.

Jeez, Dad . . . give a guy a break.

<u>Back to 1998: New York</u>

The first day of the New York trip, we behaved like the stereotypical tourists; the weekend was all about standing in the streets, gawking at the Disney-fication of Times Square, eating bagels from some hole-in-the-wall deli and saying to ourselves, "Cool! It's New York!" No wonder New Yorkers are so rude--locals can tolerate such behavior only so long before their heads implode. I'm sure New York natives would much prefer to see the throngs of tourists stuffed into harnesses and herded like goats through the city on a predictable, clearly defined route. But lacking a herding-tourists-like-goats-union, they try to scare gawkers to death instead.

Our second day in New York was June 8, 1998, otherwise known as my thirty-fifth birthday and, since it had never occurred to me that I would reach my thirty-fifth year on this planet without going insane, I decided to do something nice for myself in celebration. In the movies, there's a soundtrack to foreshadow foreboding events; in life, there's bad hair days. I thought of my friends who had just turned forty and debated following their leads: 1) parachuting out of a small plane; 2) running a marathon; 3) buying a hot car and start dating a twenty-one-year-old. I decided I'm too fearful of heights to make the plane a feasible option. That left the marathon or the car/ twenty-one-year-old options. I decided that since I used to be a runner, running another marathon would be cheating and who the hell could afford a hot car, not to mention a hot twenty-one-year-old? I briefly considered eating candy while watching other people jumping out of a plane, eating lunch in a street cafe during a marathon, or watching a porn movie about a twenty-one-year-old in a hot car, but all these options seemed too boring. What can I say? I was young and still under the misconceived notion that your birthday was a celebratory occasion. That stops once you turn forty. There's nothing more pathetic than a forty-something-year-old dragging himself into middle-age insisting that he isn't cresting the over-the-hill. Besides, sooner or later you realize that millions of other people on Earth were born on the same day. Statistics say 4,000 babies are born every minute. Happy birthday to you and the 3,999 others.

I chose to do something I knew I could do to mark the day. I trimmed my beard. Hiding myself in the bathroom of the apartment while everyone else was asleep, I revved up the beard trimmer and took stock of the fur covering my jowls. I really dislike trimming my beard, but it's better than the odd looks when the hair on your face is longer than the sparse hair on your head, and it beats shaving every day. Who was the sadist who invented the idea of a man putting a razor blade to his throat? Does that make any sense to anybody? Doesn't society frown upon playing with sharp objects?

A snip here, a snip there and the beard was shaping up nicely. Until, of course, the knock on the door made me jump. The electric beard trimmer snipped right through the jawline, giving my cheek a racing stripe.

"Are you in the shower?" Mom yelled.

"No, Ma, I was trimming the beard."

"What does it look like? Let's see it."

"Almost done. Do you want in?"

"No. Just checking."

"No sweat." I considered leaving the racing stripe, but in the end felt a reverse mutton chop was not hip nor cool, just plain stupid looking. What the hell, I thought as I shoved the machine over the rest of my face, I've always wanted a goatee anyway.

The plan for my birthday was to visit Greenwich Village. I wanted more than anything else to have a picture of myself outside the Stonewall Bar as a memento for my journal, which had become a depository of boring writing and half finished poems. I figured a few pictures of famous locales would spice it up enough to make me want to open the cover again. I had read about the Stonewall Bar, seen the documentary about its role in the Gay Rights Movement, but have never been there. This fact embarrassed me, as during my college years I was an extremely vocal civil rights activist. I also did a lot of drinking and took a lot of drugs, but for some reason I didn't connect these activities until after I turned forty and all my friends became members of the GOP.

After a late breakfast in a crowded deli, thick with the aroma of baking bread, where we all drank way too much coffee and ate too much schmear, we arrived in the Village. Schmear, I believe, is New York's retaliation against tourists. Locals don't eat "schmear", they eat cream cheese. Cream cheese costs less than half that of schmear. Do the math.

"Want to go in?" Mom asked, pointing to the Stonewall Bar.

"Nah. Just a picture. Stand together, okay?" I dug out my camera.

Just as I framed the shot, Gary and Troy disappeared through the front door of the bar.

"They're going in," Mom sounded disappointed. "Come on." She waved at me and disappeared into the bar after them. I chased after her.

Something mystical happens when a mother enters into a gay bar. She instantly morphs into "EveryMom: Fag Magnet".

The bartender smiled. "Good afternoon!" He waved at her. He ignored me.

"Hi!" Mom said, nodding.

The guys sitting on the bar stools turned in unison and toasted her, wide smiles on their faces. Mom waved back. They ignored me.

"This is a very friendly place," She whispered to me.

"Yep," I agreed. If only I could get this much attention when I came to a bar without her, I thought. Is that the secret to gay dating in the '90s? Bring your mother?

By this time, Gary and Troy had circled the place and deemed it too slow for any action and accepted the fact that they needed to join us. They hovered at the door ready to go.

"What's back there?" she asked, pointing to the black curtains pulled across the doorway at the rear of the place.

"Nothing, Ma," I said. "Let's hit the road."

If there's anything I've learned about hyper sexual establishments, it's that you never want your mother looking at the men behind the curtain.

"Let's go get my picture."

It was as I wandered down the sidewalk looking for a photogenic shot of Christopher Street that the huge display window caught her eye.

"Look at this!" she pointed. The display window sported several mannequins in various stages of undress. The one she pointed to was an androgynous figure wearing a colorfully outlandish mini-skirt, Elton John (circa-1970) sunglasses, a feather boa and a leather necklace. On its feet were eight inch platform shoes made of clear plastic, inside of which were tiny goldfish, swimming their little fins off. "Who wears those?"

"Drag queens."

"They're going to fall off their shoes and break their necks."

"It's the least of their worries."

"What's that?" she asked, pointing to the store that held the leather-clad mannequins behind the display window.

"Mannequins wearing leather."

"I can see that," she said rolling her eyes. "Duh. I mean the store. What store is that?"

"Probably one selling marital aids."

"What?"

"Sex shop." I looked at her. The perplexed look on her face touched my heart. It's the same look a forlorn animal gives you right before you stoop to pet them and they bite your face off. "You go to one of those places to buy toys, clothing and other paraphernalia for . . . spicing up a relationship."

"Oh. Have you ever been in one?"

I looked at her. "Do you really want me to answer that question?"

She thought about this a minute. "Let's go in."

"No, Ma, you cannot go in the sex shop." As a friend of mine once told me, we all know our parents have (or have had) sex in their lives. We are all aware that our parents weren't born yesterday and have a working knowledge of the human anatomy. Regardless, we don't want to discuss sex with our parents because we don't want the visual picture of our parents fornicating to forever be imprinted on our minds. Besides, I couldn't get my dad's voice out of my head: "She's your mother for Christ's sake. Take care of her. Don't get her killed!" Granted, a sex shop doesn't carry the same danger as a drive-by shooting, but I wasn't taking any chances. She might see something that could give her a heart attack.

"Why not?"

"Because, Ma, if you go in there, Dad will think I'm not taking care of you."

"Why do you worry so much about what your father is going to say?"

I hesitated for a minute, trying to decide if this was the time or place to start that conversation. Is this something she really needs to know? I was just about to make a flip comment and gloss over the topic when she let me off the hook by chuckling and grabbing my arm.

"We'll buy something for your father. That'll be fun."

"No," I turned to Gary and Troy for support. "Help!"

"I think its a great idea," Gary said.

"Me, too," Troy agreed. He took Mom by the arm and headed for the door. "Let's go."

I wedged them apart. "Let's not, okay? Lunch. We need lunch."

I turned and walked away. I took about five steps before I realized that Mom wasn't behind me. I turned just in time to see her disappearing into the sex shop, nodding thanks to Gary and Troy who stood holding the door open for her. They smiled at me, waved and followed her into the shop. I scurried after them, hoping to shield her from the worst of the marital aids, thus avoiding a lengthy and potentially embarrassing discussion as to how said devices are used. The first thing I saw was my mother standing in front of the glass display case talking to the tall, thin salesman wearing a leather harness, jock strap, and a dog collar.

I turned to the man with his ass hanging out of the chaps and nodded. "Hi."

"Hi, he quipped, before turning back to Mom.

"Come on, Mom. Let's go." I grabbed her elbow, intent on letting her walk out under her own power to retain some dignity.

"This is your mom?" The man's face broke into a huge smile and he nodded furiously at her. "That is so cool. My mom would never come into this place."

"She's not supposed to, either." I sounded more harsh than I meant to be. It wasn't his fault my mother was a horny senior citizen.

"He's mean to me," she said with a serious tone and a twinkle in her eye. "He never lets me have any fun."

"Mom," I sighed. "You've got to get out of here." I turned to the guy. "Don't sell her anything."

"Don't tell me what I can buy, I'm over twenty-one," she said. She looked into the display case and pointed. "What's that?"

"Don't tell her." I snapped.

He ignored me. "It's a cock ring."

"Oh," she nodded. "A what?"

"A cock ring," he said. "Want to see them?"

"Sure," she said, putting her purse on the counter.

"No!" I snapped at Mr. No Shirt Ass Man.

She turned to me and said, "I am not talking to you. I am talking to him." She leaned into Mr. No Shirt Ass Man and said, "Ignore him."

He chuckled as he laid the display plate on the glass counter and gently lifted the products toward Mom. "These are leather strips with snaps," he explained. "Very popular."

I try to avoid awkward circumstances like dinner parties with people I don't know, discussing hemorrhoids in public and watching a guy wearing a dog collar showing my mother cock rings. So I scurried away from them keeping a sharp eye on Mom in case she tried to move further into the den of adult treasures. You never know when a running tackle may be necessary. When it comes to shopping, she's the National League champion; if Cro-magnon man had "shopping" as the requirement to be clan chief, we'd all be living in the basement of Tiffany's today. There's no evidence to suggest that cock rings would be any different than diamond rings in her mind.

"Your mother is hysterical," Gary said from beside me. "I love her."

"Thanks and I'm going to hurt you for this."

"She's an adult, Dave."

"No she's not, she's my mother."

Gary and Troy giggled and shook their heads. Those two were getting way too much enjoyment from this. They stepped backwards through the rack of woman's erotic panties chuckling to themselves as they hunkered down to watch Mom's adventure through the voyeur glass. I paced behind a rack of overpriced nighties, trying to appear casual. When I looked up again, I saw Mr. No-Shirt Ass Man placing the tray of cock rings into the glass display case, but Mom was nowhere to be seen.

"Where did my mom go?" I asked Mr No Shirt Ass Man.

"She went that way," pointing behind me into the bowels of the store. "You're lucky. My mom isn't half this fun."

"She's not supposed to be fun, she's my mother." Why the hell didn't these people understand the seriousness of this situation? If other moms wanted to explore the wide world of cock-rings, vibrators and anal ticklers, knock 'em dead. Go Gloria Steinem. But for God's sake, don't take my mother.

I caught sight of her at the top of the spiral staircase that lead to the basement.

"MOM!" I shouted. Shoppers looked up; more out of curiosity of a possible new sex game than annoyance, I'm sure. Gary and Troy chuckled at me from lingerie. Mom ignored me. I dashed to the staircase and caught her elbow just as her foot hit the first step.

"Don't go down there," I said.

"Why? What's down there?"

"The fun stuff." Gary and Troy suddenly appeared at her side, their hands on her shoulders, urging her into the dark basement. That's the moment I decided that they were evil and must be destroyed. "Mom, really, there are things down there which defy description. Things you have never seen before and hopefully will die having never seen them."

Mom's eyes lit up, flashing JACKPOT.

"I'll take you down," Gary said. Mom took his outstretched arm. I burst between them and pried them apart.

"We're leaving," I said.

"Seriously, David," she looked at me. "I'm curious and you never let me have any fun." Then with glee she pointed over my shoulder, "Look! A sale!" With that, she jogged over to the erotic bras.

Several minutes later, I had the three of them safely back on the street. At the time I was relieved to have my mother out of the den of depravity. It was only later that I realized I am living through one of the signs of the Apocalypse: I now considered the streets of New York a Safe Zone.

"Mom," I tried to sound as stern as I could, "do not tell Dad you went to a sex shop."

"That was a very interesting place," she said.

"Mom, I'm serious. Please do not tell Dad you went to a sex shop. He'll think I'm irresponsible and not taking care of you."

"He will not."

"Please, Ma. I don't want him to worry about us."

"Yeah, yeah, all right," she waved me aside as if I were a bug.

Hours and God knows how many dollars later, the four of us returned to the rented apartment rooms exhausted: Mom from splurging at every hole-in-the-wall boutique she could find and me from chasing her around Manhattan. I didn't know where she got her energy, but I hope I have half as much when I get to be her age. I threw some packages onto the floor of the living room as Gary and Troy threw themselves onto the hide-a-bed and picked up the TV remote.

"What the hell are you two doing?" I demanded. They stared blankly at me pretending they didn't understand what I was talking about.

"If you can't play nicely with my mom, you can't come with us tomorrow."

"Dave, don't you think you're overreacting just a bit?" Gary said.

"I don't care. Promise me, no sex shops."

"Dave, she's a lot of fun--"

"What's next? Buying crack on the street corner? How about taking her to a whorehouse while we're at it?"

"She has two kids. She knows what sex is."

"I'll ditch you two. I swear to God."

"I still don't understand your problem," Troy said clicking through the channels.

"My father-"

"Isn't here," he reminded me. "Your mother wants a vacation, Dave. You're worse than a nun. Really, what are you protecting her from?"

I hate logical questions.

"Tomorrow will be easier for you," Gary promised, "we have tickets to that play."

"Something mom-friendly?"

They shrugged. "I think so. It's called *When Pigs Fly*. How bad can it be?"

Satisfied that my mother's future held only the G-rated parts of New York City, I headed into the bedroom to give Mom the stockpile of purchases. I entered just as Mom, sitting on the edge of the bed with the phone tucked into the crook of her neck, exclaimed, "David took me to a gay sex shop!"

After a slight pause, she continued, "Okay." She held out the phone to me. "Your father wants to talk to you."

I grimaced. Here comes the "you're irresponsible" speech. "Hey, Pop."

"What in the hell are you doing?!" His voice sounded an octave higher than normal.

"What?" When one feels guilty, one should always try acting innocent unless directed otherwise.

"You know damn well what. I told you, she was your responsibility!" His voice went from strained to forced.

"Well . . . she wandered off."

"Wandered off?" he said. "How can a fifty-four year old woman wander off?"

"She's very . . . wandery . . ."

"You need to take care of your mother," he said. "What's next? Taking her to buy dope?"

Proof that neurotics are a product of nature, not nurture. "No, Dad. Really. It's all good." Like I would know where to find dope.

"Bring her back to me in one piece! Put her back on."

For the rest of the night I fumed. Why did I get yelled at? It's not my fault I have a curious, sex-obsessed mother. She's an adult woman! What was I supposed to do? Tackle her and hogtie her? Anyway, she started the escapade with her, "Oh, let's go see the inside of a sex shop" thing.

"What did your father say?" she asked out of the darkness as we lay in bed later that night. Her voice sounded thick with sleep.

"He's mad at me because you went into the sex shop," I whined. "Thanks for getting me in trouble." When innocent doesn't work, try whining. It never worked as a kid, but, hey! I'm older now and have more practice at whining.

"Tough toe nails, Tony," She said. "Today was really fun. I had a good time. Thanks for bringing me with you."

I didn't respond. Innocence, whining AND the silent treatment -- she was getting the entire arsenal from me this time. She remained silent. Good. Maybe she would feel bad that she got me in trouble with Dad. I let her stew on that a few minutes before I followed it up.

"Night, Mom."

She was fast asleep. Moms really knows how to hurt sons.

***

"I notice you didn't have your wedding ring on," my Mom said, pointing to my left hand.

"Yeah," I murmur, "I finally got to the point in my life where I could bring myself to take it off."

"Oh," she says, then gives me The Look.

Thanks to all the new theories of childrearing that rule out disciplining your children due to possible injuries to their self-esteem, I'm not sure how many youth today can identify with The Look. Ask any of us over the age of thirty and we all can tell you tales of how The Look molded our childhood. Sometimes referred to as the "Mom Look" and the "Mom Eyes", it has the effect of an emotional nuclear explosion. (I've even met one man from India who calls it "Mom's Devil Eyes". Apparently in India there is a direct line from Satan to a Mother's psyche. As if there would be any doubt.) There's no avoiding The Look. The Look carries within it a magical ability to cause grown men to change into babbling children, or an independent woman to question her choice to keep her maiden name. I suspect if Charles Manson's mother had been around to apply The Look, Roman Polanski would still be living in Hollywood. If we could bottle The Look, society could save a fortune on police protection. For those of you under thirty, or lacking the experience of encountering The Look, The Look is a sideways glance from your mother which is a combination of inquisitive prying, acknowledgement, pity and condemnation for something you may (or may not) have done.

I could feel her eyes boring into my skull. Because I was raised with one of the Master Lookers, I knew Mom was expecting some kind of response from me about her wedding ring comment. Not a total soul-baring tell-all tale worthy of the National Enquirer, but a response of some sort was expected.

"We split," I said simply.

She nodded and continued giving me The Look.

"He didn't want to leave Seattle," I said. This was the truth. My five-year relationship was coming to a close over the simple fact I wanted to continue my education into graduate school and he didn't want to move away from his comfort zone of friends and family. I could understand it if he was a multi-millionaire business tycoon with a staff depending upon his involvement, but he was unemployed. His most pressing commitment was to *Days Of Our Lives*.

"I wanted more and he didn't, I guess," I said.

"Really?" She knew there was more to the story.

"I asked him to come with me. He said no. I had to make a choice: continue school or not. I didn't want to make that 'not' choice." She nodded in understanding.

I continued, although I don't know why I felt the need, "It pisses me off. Why do people say 'I love you', when what they mean is, 'I love you under these circumstances'? Why don't they just say that right off the bat and get it over with?"

She pointed to the theatre entrance. "Are they letting us in now?"

"I'm baring my soul and you're wondering about grabbing your seat in the theatre?"

"I don't want to miss the curtain. Your self-loathing will still be here after it's over."

She was right, of course. The patrons were flowing into the lobby already. That's one thing about my mom--her powers of dual-tasking are off the charts. I wonder if it's an X-chromosome thing, or if it's training from the days of laundromats, stick-shift cars and children on your hips?

As I man, I guess I'll never know.

***

The theatre's design made every seat a good seat. Mom, Gary, Troy and I sat a few rows back, center of the house. A tidy, humorous piece, *When Pigs Fly* was more of a musical review than a play. A thin storyline barely wide enough to hold the series of comedic songs and vignettes was just enough to keep the story flowing. Mom thoroughly enjoyed it.

I, on the other hand, laughed through clenched fists. Primarily playing to a gay audience, the entire show was filled with innuendoes and tongue-in-cheek jokes that I found hysterical but left Mom asking questions I would prefer not to answer.

"Cruising . . . like up and down Main Street in a 1950s' Chevy?" she whispered.

"Cruising . . . as in looking for a brief sexual encounter." I whispered back.

"Lube . . . Jiffy Lube?"

"Lube . . . Vaseline, K.Y. Jelly, sexual lubrication."

"Oh! Like the sex shop!" She sounded excited as she put the pieces of the puzzle together. Me--not so excited. *K-Y Jelly* and *Mom* were three words and a hyphen I never wanted to put into a sentence together.

Mom was quite capable of dealing with bawdy humor, but I am incapable of explaining bawdy humor to my mom. Especially when history has already shown that every bawdy reference in her ear comes out of her mouth to my father who instantly hunts me down like a rabid dog and accuses me of turning my mom into a pervert.

In the second act, however, when the Cupid character pondered to himself whether to aim high for the "TOP" or low for the "BOTTOM", I ignored her when she leaned over and whispered, "What's that mean?"

Some roads I don't want to travel.

I thought I had succeeded with my plan to keep her isolated from sexual innuendos and content until later that night in the rented apartment when she called from the other room, "David!" Then, as I stood on the threshold, she held the phone to me and said, "Your father wants to talk to you."

***

"Where are we going?" I've asked her for the third or fourth time.

"To Macy's. HELLO! I told you that."

She told me lots of things so far today. Like how she wanted to go into Tiffany's to look around and wound up talking to the saleswoman about diamonds. The poor woman thought she had a rich old widow and was beginning to foam at the mouth before it became apparent that neither Mom nor I had enough money to pay for the cab.

"What are you going to get in Macy's?"

"Duh!" She rolled her eyes. "We can't go to New York and pass up Macy's! Don't you watch the parade?"

"No."

"See?" She pointed to a nearby display window. "Oh! Pretty!" Then, moving on again, she continued. "If you watched the parade, you'd know Macy's."

"Ma, I know Macy's," I defended myself. "I don't know why Macy's is so important."

I followed her into Macy's and she headed directly for the Men's Department, where huge signs advertised SALE SALE SALE. When it comes to shopping, Mom has a radar that rivals a dolphin's ability to find a crab under six feet of rubble.

I stood, bored, watching people wander aimlessly amongst racks of clothes. She flipped through shirts, making strange faces at each one. "No. No. GOD NO! This is nice. This isn't bad . . ."

"What are you looking for?"

"Here. Try this on." She thrust a shirt at me. I slipped it over my T-shirt. "No! Try it on. Duh! I need to see if it fits."

I lumbered over to the dressing room and tried it on. I modeled it under unnatural florescent lights. She nodded. "Good. Take it off." By the time I exited the dressing room, she had wandered back to the large table bearing the words HALF PRICE!

"Which tie do you like better?" She asked, laying down a green Pierre Cardin shirt still in the protective packaging and holding up three ties.

I glanced at all three. I hate ties. Between the holding of a blade against one's throat and tying a knot around one's neck, I wonder how men survived this long. The fashion police are constantly trying to kill us. I pointed to the least boring of the three.

"I like this one. It's nice. Come on." She spun and headed to the register.

A hyper-friendly salesman with big teeth checked us out. "Having a good day?"

"Oh, yes!" Mom responded. "We're headed to Ellis Island."

"Oh," the man responded, although I couldn't distinguish if it was out of excitement or the hope of getting a larger sale, ergo a huge commission.

"We saw . . . let's see . . ." Mom thought. "We saw the Empire State Building earlier this morning. Have you ever been there?"

The man nodded and told her the price of the purchase. Mom ignored him.

"It was so nice! Just like in that movie with Cary Grant. You know the one where he is supposed to meet her on the roof of the Empire State Building?"

"That was *Sleepless in Seattle*," I said.

"It was a Cary Grant movie first," she said. The man repeated the price. Mom ignored him. "They always remake the really good movies."

"I think the guy wants his money, Ma."

"I know," she said, "I'm just trying to be social."

"It's New York," I whispered. "They aren't real 'social' people."

"You're just like your father," she sighed, pocketing the credit card.

The man practically threw the purchase at us and turned to help another customer. As we headed out to the sidewalk, I turned to Mom.

"So . . . Ellis Island next?"

She nodded. "I can't wait. It is supposed to be great." I held the door for her as we headed out into the throng. She handed me the bag.

"Here," she said shoving past me, "now you have a decent shirt to wear to work. And--" she checked her watch "--less than twenty minutes."

"Is that why you bought this?" I asked. She nodded. "Why didn't you just say so?"

"Because all you do is bitch about shopping," she said, getting her bearings on the street. "Now you have a decent shirt, didn't spend all morning hanging out with your irritating mother shopping AND you can tell all your students you have a shirt from Macy's."

"Wow." I tried to think of something to say that wouldn't sound trite. I failed.

She sniffed. "You dress like a slob. You need a decent shirt and tie."

I resisted the urge to groan. I only wear a shirt and tie when I teach, and then it's only under duress. Most of the time, it's jeans and T-shirts.

"Your father always said you dressed like a slob, too. You have no nice clothes." This was stated as fact, no room for discussion.

"Thanks, Mom. It was just so expensive."

"Stop bitching about shopping, wear the Goddamn shirt and stop complaining about being thirty-five and traveling with your mother."

"I'm not complaining!"

"Well, don't say I never gave you nothing."

"No problem." I pulled out the map. "Which way?"

She shrugged. "I don't care. I'm easy. I ain't cheap, but I'm easy."

RELATED TANGENT #2
Free Writing Exercise from August 1, 2007

I believe in mental telepathy. Not necessarily the "woo-woo-I-can-see-inside-your-mind-because-I'm-a-gypsy-fortune-teller" kind of telepathy, but a different, almost spiritual kind of mental connection between people who share a deep emotional bond.

Don't misunderstand me, I wish I was blessed with the "woo-woo-I-can-see-inside-your-mind-because-I'm-a-gypsy-fortune-teller" kind of superpower, but it has never been one of my talents. I wanted that talent, though. I used to lie in the field near my childhood home watching clouds and fantasizing about reading minds, moving objects with my thoughts, or using my psychic prowess to rip apart every kid in my school who taunted me for being fat. I was one of those creepy kids who ran around the house pretending to be Superman. For the most part, my parents rolled their eyes and ignored the beach towel cape, until one day when I was about six. I morphed into Superman and flew myself through the storm door window, sending shards of glass everywhere and giving my mother the scare of a lifetime. I don't know how I avoided cutting myself to shreds on the splinters, but I did. Since then, Mom always shunned the "hands on" part of flying. That annoying law of physics called gravity *took precedence over my law of magical thinking.*

I believe in telepathy for a couple reasons. First, you ask any scientist and they'll tell you that the average human uses less than 10% of his/her brain, which begs the question. "What do we do with the other 90%, besides show an unusual interest in nosing our way into other people's lives via Judge Judy, Jerry Springer *and and US magazine?" Granted, any imbecile can see that most of humanity uses only a fraction of their brains just by driving down the freeway. Directional signals? HA! And don't get me started on the idiots in the fast lane who plod along ten mph under the speed limit because they're busy chatting on the cell phone. I think humanity needs to revisit this idea of forced sterilization.*

Another reason I believe in the kind of "emotional bond" mental telepathy is because I hang out with women, most of them mothers. More appropriately, mothers hang out with me. There's nothing so attractive to women as gay men. It's a symbiotic relationship; they live vicariously through us and we get to be reminded that the label "loser" applies to men both gay and straight. So be forewarned if your mother is still alive -- she's telling me your secrets. Your mom may not know you did hundreds of drugs, or you lost track of how many people you've slept with, but she knows you're a slut and a druggie.

I have experienced this type of mental telepathy three times in my life. Afterwards, I remember having a new appreciation for being acutely normal, as none of the three experiences moved me into the "superhero" category. Once was when I had a mental vision of my friend's room in her house where I had never been. The second was when my biological sister went into labor with her eldest child. The third was the day my father died.

I worked in a call center at the time which had a strict "no cell phone" policy. I had forgotten to turn mine off, so when it rang in the middle of my shift, I hurriedly snatched it out of my backpack. As I pressed the button to turn it off, I saw that it was Mom. A chill went through me. I felt light-headed. I suddenly wanted to throw up. I knew she was calling because my father was dead. I don't know how I knew, but I knew. I knew it as surely as you can recite your social security number when asked.

The phone had powered down by now and I heard a co-worker asking for my help. I left my cubicle to take care of some business, finishing up about thirty minutes later. Trembling, I told my boss I had a personal call to make and turned on my phone. When it booted up, the screen flashed my sister's number, so instead of calling Mom, I hit REDIAL. It ended up that my sister was the one who told me my father had suffered a heart attack in the garage. Mom had found him; his lips already turning blue.

This story falls under the category of Twilight Zone *because Mom says she didn't call me that day. My sister agrees. True, the stress of the situation could have clouded Mom's memory, but there was another odd fact to consider--there was no trace of Mom's call in my cell phone's call history. Still, the image of my mom's phone number popping up on my cell's display screen remains branded in my mind. I can see the cute cartoonish picture that lit up when her call came in. There was no message on my voice mail, despite the fact that my mother would rather be plowed down by a speeding bus than ignore an opportunity to talk uninterrupted. For any of those people who want scientific validation for everything under the sun, I have no explanation for what happened that day other than a psychic flash from Mom to me. I believe in mental telepathy because I believe in the bond between mother and child.*

The '70s: Minds of the Lost

When I was young, I was not the usual run-of-the-mill hesitantly shy child that you see peeking around the corner and makes you smile because they're so cute. I was the freakishly weird child that looked at you and you itched. I was the kid who read *Jaws* (I always was an advanced reader) and then refused to swim in the neighborhood pool just in case sharks acquired the ability to breath chlorine. Whenever the family camped, I would ask my parents about the history of the campsite, prying into the possibility that we were headed for certain death as we cranked open our JayCo "pop-up" camper in a location inhabited by axe-wielding murderers. My parents would roll their eyes and remind me that "Lightning doesn't strike the same place twice." I believed them and went happily skipping down the road of life seeking out disastrous relationships and stepping on the sidewalk cracks thinking, "I'm safe! I'm safe! The destruction has already happened!"

Imagine my surprise when, years later, I read the NASA-STI (Scientific and Technological Information) website:

Contrary to popular misconception, lightning often strikes the same place twice. Certain conditions are just ripe for a bolt of electricity to come zapping down; and a lightning strike is powerful enough to do a lot of damage wherever it hits. NASA created the Accurate Location of Lightning. Strikes technology to determine the ground strike point of lightning and revent electrical damage in the immediate vicinity of the Space Shuttle launch pads at Kennedy Space Center.

***

I should be thankful that nothing ever happened to me during those carefree years of youth, but this discovery posed more questions than answers, such as why NASA doesn't invent something important--like "Accurate Location of Lost Youth" technology. Or "Potential Loser Boyfriend" finder. Life is so unfair at times.

So when I flew to Iowa in 2009 for the writer's workshop, I had a hunch that some devastation would strike while I was there. The prior summer, Iowa was hit by a flood which closed the university, crippled the town of Iowa City and left water standing on the street for months. This act of God would mark the region for yet another natural disaster, I was sure of it.

So it came as no surprise that after the opening night preamble and the enthusiastic would-be writers headed to the classrooms, that the sky became ominously dark. Suddenly, the wind began to whip around the buildings at a breakneck speed, sending the trees bending under the assault. Then the tornado warning siren blared and the entire hoard of students scrambled to the basement, where we sat on the cold tile floors waiting for the "All clear" siren, or a Kansas farmhouse to whirl by, trapped inside a tornado--whichever came first.

In an attempt to keep the class moving forward, the teacher-- wanting to fan the spark of creativity--asked about a time when we remembered feeling "pure joy". She may as well have asked me to remove my spleen with an oven mitt and a butter knife. "Pure joy"? How about 99% joy? What is joy, anyway? Trying to remember when you felt "joy" is like trying to remember a specific heartbeat, or time you stubbed your toe in the dark on the way to the bathroom after a night of one-too-many beers. I don't remember feelings of pure hate, pure horror or pure happiness, either. So when I was asked about "pure joy", what could I say? The closest I've felt is the occasional nudge of something called gratitude. Was it really possible that anyone could single out a specific emotion from the myriad of conflicting, convoluted emotions we feel everyday? Should we expect ourselves to do so? Things that are a part of life so inextricably connected to the everyday ups and downs become a part of who we are and mold how we see life.

As I sat on the floor contemplating "pure joy", an epiphany came to me: life is NOT like a box of chocolates as Forest Gump claimed. Life is like having a bad case of the chicken pox.

On the side of my left eye, right where the two lids meet, I have a slight indentation in the shape of an oval. It's not so pronounced that it looks like a third eye, but to anyone standing closer than five feet, the mark is obvious. I always noticed it, of course, but for some reason I never asked my mom about it. The mystery of childhood-- the world could end over a dropped popsicle, but a facial deformation can be forgotten as long as there are no mirrors around. One day, my mom happened to be walking past me when I was thinking about this mark on my face. She waved the story off, sighed, and told me that when I was a child, my sister and I got the chicken pox. Not being content to be properly horrified by the growth of strange red dots on my face, I set about picking at them. Despite her warnings that it would hurt, or that my face would fall off, I continued to pick at the scabs until she was too frustrated to yell at me to stop. The mark was the remnant of that early act of defiance and exploration.

She shrugged, "I told you to stop."

"Ma, I was . . . what? Five?"

"See? You should have listened to me."

At the tender and rebellious age of five, I was too young to remember being sick, so I can't validate this story. It makes sense, though, as my parents are the type who, for some reason, never got a photo of me with red splotches all over my face although they seemed to have had the time to capture every other embarrassing moment of my childhood on celluloid. I don't know how this Kodak moment passed them by. The chicken pox portion of the story is true, because I have this glorious mark near my eye. The chicken pox incident was nothing more than a moment in time that happened to me without fanfare or DVD, yet the proof of my scar remains. Emotions are that way, too. We may not remember when we feel joy or sadness, but the stories behind the emotions stay with us like scars on our psyches.

I've heard it said that "joy" is a collection of moments of contentment that make up a happy life. I don't know if that's true or if it's a device invented by Hallmark for sentimental blackmail. I do know that during those times I feel that life can't be any worse than being a forty-six year old, pudgy, balding guy; or those times that I feel the world closing in around me, scattered pictures of my life's moments of contentment play like a movie in my mind and they make me smile. I forget for a moment that life sucks.

Directly or indirectly, many of these memories involve my family, and those mental scenarios rattle around my mind like a can of pop that escaped the easy-to-carry cardboard case. Strewn throughout my lifetime like frosting roses over the top of a cake, the memories are evenly spaced, but with that ubiquitous clump in one of the corners. In my life's story, those roses often involve my mother, Penny, and the clump in the corner are the times we traveled together. Frustrating at times, annoying at others and always unpredictable, the snapshots of joy hang around the fringes of my mind, clinging to the walls of reminiscence waiting for me to dive in with a spoon screaming, "Mine! Mine! All mine!"

Another epiphany hit me while I sat on that cold tile floor in the basement (epiphanies come to me like pigeon on a summer day--in flocks of scattered, dirty chaos that everybody ignores). This new epiphany was about the effects of these emotionally-laden experiences--we remember the people who shared these experiences with us more than we remember the experiences. We feel joy and pain because we are social animals, we homo sapiens--and the stories of the people in our lives is what shapes those lives. I'm not talking about the whole storybook tale of a life filled with children, a wife and a house with a picket fence. (We know that myth was created by Wall Street for the sole purpose of selling a zillion greeting cards.) What people leave behind is more than children, the family Bible and boxes of stuff gathering dust. It's the emotions that memories of people evoke in us that is the lasting legacy.

Let me give you an example of what I mean. The best gifts I've ever received were short stories that a friend of mine wrote every Christmas. He would print these tales onto textured paper, then roll the stories into a scroll and tie them off with a ribbon. I don't have those stories today. I have nothing of his personal belongings that I could call mementos. However, every time I think of him, I remember the giddy happiness I felt when he handed me his Christmas scroll and the warmth that flowed through me after reading these heart warming tales. I suppose, then, this is what "joy" means: joy is the feeling we have when someone we care for tells us that, for a moment, we had their undivided attention.

My problem is that I tend to ride the middle of things, whether it be politics, an argument, or Coke vs. Pepsi. I spent long years dancing close enough to people to feel the pull of their personality, but far enough away that it doesn't hurt when we part. Despite this odd emotional tug-of-war, there is a shelf in my mind where I stack mental snapshots about people. I wish I could say I mentally peruse them because I'm a compassionate and tender guy, but the truth is I only look back on my life when those snippets of memory decide to leap off the shelf and throw themselves in my face. (Honestly, who really knows when those little buggers will come to haunt us?) Getting off the middle isn't easy. It takes something big. It takes something so full of emotional significance that the force of it pushes you off center.

The "joyous memory" snapshot that came to the forefront of my mind while I sat on the floor in Iowa waiting for the Kansas farmhouse to hurl by was an old memory: I'm in New England, visiting my grandparents. It is sometime around 1973 and I'm about ten years old; old enough to know that my grandparents live in Rhode Island and young enough to be oblivious to the fact that I should be embarrassed that they live in a trailer park. The gray skies stack thick overhead, blotting out the sunlight and the winds bite as they rip over my skin.

My grandfather and I stand on the jagged rocks of the shore of the North Atlantic. He is a rough guy; the kind of man who would scare me if I saw him coming towards me on the street. Tall--of course, he was probably only 5'10", but when you're ten, everyone over four feet is tall--wrinkles, thick cigar in his fingers and stubble on his grizzled face. His voice is rough from years of smoking and heavy drinking.

Seagulls scream overhead, water droplets cling to my coat and the frigid ocean sloshes over the rocky shore onto my leg. This is exciting for me as well as a tad frightening. I'm from suburban Chicago. The lakes along northern Illinois don't "slosh" nor do the get whipped up from the winds. They sort of lie there playing opossum to unsuspecting children and water skiers. It's only when people play in them that they rear up and attack. New England waters blatantly tell visitors they are unwelcome; Chicago waters betray them.

"Cup your hand and put the water in it." He is insistent. I do this.

"Now," he says, "taste the water." I don't understand. Aren't we only supposed to drink water from the tap?

I'm not sure why I'm doing this, but I do. I gag. I spit. I'm grossed out. It's like swallowing a mouthful of salt.

"That's the taste of the sea," Grandpa says with a chuckle. "Never forget it. She covers most of the world and she's a finicky lady. Treat her with respect and even then she may kill you."

He reaches down and grabs my hand. I eagerly accept his help and he half pulls me, half lifts me from the rocks, now slippery with the seawater of this "Lady Ocean" who apparently is a bitch.

As he helps me over the last couple of rocks, he leans over and hugs me fiercely. His breath smells of smoke, but it doesn't bother me. He is warm in the chilly wind and familiar amongst these unfamiliar surroundings.

I look over his shoulder as he hugs me. I see my mom and dad standing near the rocky incline on the smooth pavement of the parking lot. Mom is pointing to something out on the horizon. Dad stands behind her, nodding. I see her lips move but can't hear anything. Finally, she lowers her arm and Dad reaches up and puts his hand on her shoulder. They look like a commercial from one of the Saturday morning cartoons I love to watch: loving couple planning the birth of their child, or some such 1960s' propaganda.

The moment with my parents lasted a few seconds; hardly noticeable to the passer-by. But in my mind, those seconds froze as solid as water in a pond in January. The picture in my mind makes me feel warm, despite the chill inside the university's basement.

Music and the Mirror

Michael Jackson died in June of 2009, while I was in Iowa City at the Writer's Workshop, just days after our tornado scare. Normally, the death of celebrity is something that I have no interest in thinking about, discussing or using brain cells to remember. The reason Michael Jackson's death struck a chord was because, a) I had expected one natural disaster, not a natural disaster AND the death of a celebrity; and b) I had just hung up with Mom (we were arguing about which state was more humid: Tennessee or Iowa. I let her win with Tennessee. I still think it was Iowa.). Our family always used MJ as a touchstone for telling people where we lived.

"Cary," one of us would tell a stranger when asked where we lived.

"Gary? Indiana?" was the response heard 90% of the time. "Like Michael Jackson?"

We would roll our eyes. "No! They're from Gary. We're from Cary. With a 'C'." It was as if the King of Pop existed solely so we could refer to him when giving directions to our hometown.

On the day MJ died, I had settled into a booth in one of the local watering holes called The Mill. I had just told a fellow writing student, Chris, whom I met in class two years ago, and Bart Yates, our teacher, about the philosophical discussion with my mom. They agreed with me on both counts: Iowa is much more humid than Tennessee, and a son should always let his mother win arguments. Just as we put that conversation to bed, the waitress came around asking for drinks when Chris blurted out "Michael Jackson's dead."

"Which one?" secretly hoping it was the right wing talk show host. I know, I'm evil. So kill me.

"You know . . . the singer," our waitress said with a high pitched laugh and a roll of the eyes at Chris.

"Bullshit." It's my standard answer to anything that surprises me. There must be a social commentary about people's inability to trust in their fellow man hidden within my standard answer, but I'll leave that for the therapists to figure out. Therapists and poets, because in truth, the poets do a better job at understanding human nature. Therapists have too much education to be smart.

I turned to the waitress, "Well?"

"Yeah!" She seemed too happy about this news. "That's why we've been playing all his old videos." She pointed to the TV over the bar. Sure enough, *Billie Jean* was flashing across the screen, with the lighted sidewalks and MJ dressed in a trench-coat. The enticing part of Michael Jackson's videos is the stories they tell. I love a good story and when one is put to music well--what more do you want?

"He is the third," she continued. "MJ, Farrah Fawcett and that other guy who used to do the talk show."

"Ed McMahon," Bart said, turning to me. "It was Ed McMahon."

"Yeah," she said, "him." She giggled, took our orders and left.

I turned to Bart. "The other guy who used to do the talk show?"

He shrugged. "We're old, my friend."

I knew that. There is nothing like taking a class with a gaggle of twenty-somethings to remind you just how old you are. I watched the TV in the corner. By now, Michael flashed his shiny new glove, grabbed his crotch--again--and the herd of effeminate gang members echoed "Beat it." He used to be cool. How did society move from COOL to OVER so quickly?

Maybe Dad was onto something when he said, "Never trust a guy who wears one glove and sings *Beat It*."

After seeing the "ancient" Michael Jackson videos of the "really old fifty-year-old", I needed some perspective. Did my apathetic attitude towards music come from a childhood trauma that I suppressed? Perhaps tainted by a bad experience with concerts during my years as a toddler? It could have been either, since my first concert memory featured both Barry Manilow and Mom.

The concert happened sometime in the1970s when everything was cool for the first time; wild colors, wild parties, platform shoes and Barry. Years later in a Greenwich Village store that features clothes for drag queens, Mom and I were to stumble across the same fashions. Only this time, the thing that made the artifacts cool was not in their newness, but the retro-pseudo quirkiness of them. It seems the cycle is in fashion, grossly out of fashion, forgotten, favored by drag-queens, taken up by urban youth, cool again. I've noticed most pop culture owes its popularity to drag queens.

The power of Barry was damn near tangible in those pre-MTV/drive-by-shooting/crotch grabbing days. He was on the radio, TV, movies and--most importantly for my friend Jill--on Mom's favorite artists list.

"Your mom listens to Barry Manilow?" Her eyes grew wide and her voice accelerated to a pitch that only dogs could hear. I nodded.

Then, with one huge change in octave, she clapped her hands together. "HE'S COMING TO CHICAGO!" Then, with all the quiet earnestness at her sixteen-year-old disposal, whispered, "Can you get your mom to take us?"

I knew I should have been equally as eager to go to a concert, but the idea of sitting in a huge arena surrounded by strangers listening to music that I could hear for free on the radio didn't excite me. Besides, I had never been to a concert before and didn't know how excited I should get while still maintaining my image of being cool. Told you I bordered on the pathetic side.

Peer pressure being the heart-and-soul of high school, it became imperative that I persuade my mom to take us, as Jill's mom was not remotely qualified for this special honor. Jill's mom was rich, dressed in clothes from Saks Fifth Avenue and drove a European import. My mom had a job, dressed in clothes from JCPenney and drove a station wagon. More importantly, my mom had a fan club. "Your mom is cool!" my friends would all say and then flock to my house where they promptly ignored me and spent their time chatting up Mom. I'm not sure if I had friends because I deserved them, or because my friends thought my parents were a vacation from their home life. This fascination would fade with time, however, as not only are high school kids fickle, maturation has a way of making the COOLNESS factor die a miserable death when the "DO YOUR PARENTS HAVE LIQUOR WE CAN STEAL?" factor becomes increasingly more important.

Convincing Mom was much easier than I thought. One morning as I readied myself for school, I nonchalantly said, "Oh, yeah, we were talking about Barry Manilow coming to Chicago."

"Ohhh! I like him!" Mom said. I think she was pouring coffee into a thermos.

"Yeah, there's this friend at school who wants to go see him."

"That sounds like fun! I'll go with you." Like that, we had a ride. Things with Mom have a habit of just . . . happening.

The next thing I know, we have four tickets and I'm in the car driving to the amphitheater with Mom, her friend and Jill. The entire night was spent standing up to applaud, sitting down, jumping back up, straining over the heads of the tall people in front of us and then doing it all over again. It was vaguely reminiscent of a Catholic high mass. Overall, the experience struck me as strange and did little to ignite the adolescent passion for live music. The music could easily be heard over the radio much more clearly than in a stadium full of screaming people. The Cokes were a heck of a lot more expensive than if we bought them at the store. The T-shirts cost a small fortune, too. It all seemed so . . . wasteful. I decided that I wasn't the concert type. Maybe it's genetic or something; my parents never went to concerts, either.

The memory that lingers, though, despite this lackluster experience, would act as both a precursor to the relationship with my mother and a set the stage for my future expectations from people in general. During the show, Mom sat two seats over from me. As Barry came out to sing the final encore, I happened to glance over. Mom stood with her hands raised in the air, swaying to the music and singing along. This shocked me. Parents did this kind of thing? Don't most moms bitch about the laundry, throw shoes outside if their kids forgot to pick them up and lecture endlessly about responsibility? Moms do not act like crazed teenagers rocking out to Barry Manilow. But here my mother was, more excited than I. She was having a great time. She was happy. Several days later, I commented on her crazed unmom-like behavior.

She said. "I've always wanted to go to concerts. Your dad doesn't like the crowds, so we never went."

That was the first time I realized that just because people have a couple kids doesn't mean that they're grown up; my parents were human. I began to understand that maybe--just maybe--they had things they dreamed of doing, the same as I did. In retrospect, it seems like an odd thing to realize, but for a sixteen-year-old, any moment spent thinking about others instead of one's self is a feat. This realization would stick with me until years later, when the opportunity to travel with my mom took on a new, adult form.

The other realization that had long lasting effects happened after the show. Our cohort followed the crowd outside and stood waiting for the limo carrying Barry to pull away from the stadium. Despite the assurances that, "Barry has left the building", the throng milled about the driveway, many with autograph books in hand. Mom wasted no time pushing to the front of the crowd and stood staring at the huge garage door, waiting to see if it would open and reveal Barry behind the windows. Eventually the door did open and the limo did pull out from the darkened garage. Then it sped past all of us, the only evidence of Barry being a partially opened rear window from which an arm appeared, waving. As quickly as it appeared, it disappeared around the corner and out of sight.

As we walked back to the parking lot, Mom turned to her friend and I heard her say, "I like him. I don't care if he is gay, he's good."

The words hit me like a wall of ice water. Gay? Barry? Good? What the hell?

This statement and the questions it raised haunted me for the next couple years as I matriculated through high school, matured into young adulthood and started to explore my own sexuality.

But I always stayed in love with Barry; to this day I can't turn off the radio in the middle of one of his songs. Told you I was pathetic.

***

Do people understand that memories are powerful things? Powerful not only because of the rich history woven into them, but because as we grow older, their power changes exponentially. Time doesn't shed new light upon old family baggage. Time gives them the seed to ferment, allowing them to mature into memories far more potent than the truth ever was. Sometimes the years add strength to what we remember and the past becomes more potent than when the actual event occurred. Those pickled memories carry a kernel of the truth, but it is our own dark imagination that drinks in these fermented memories and becomes intoxicated with warped facts, so "Uncle Jerk-off beat his kids" becomes, "Oh, Uncle Jerk-Off wasn't so bad . . . he only beat people with wooden spoons" or "Oh, Aunt Hysteria was a crazy ass, bi-polar, maniac who murdered one-eyed goats on the full moon." Just like everything else, memory is susceptible to manipulation. When the memories are something dark from the past, they carry a legacy with them. Every family's tales lay dusty and faded on shelves of the past. Finding them is easy. Reading them is not.

Most of my early memories involve traveling with the family. (Don't you wish that memories from your childhood were printed on the same paper as the old One-Step cameras? Then you could be certain that, eventually, they would become brittle with age and just disintegrate into ash. The human brain may be wondrous in its composition, but it sure sucks when you're trying to forget something.) I would be reading, crammed in the backseat of a blue Chevy station wagon hauling the Jayco trailer, my sister seated behind my mom and I behind my dad. My sister irritated me because she existed. Dad irritated me because he listened to that twangy, nasal country western music of Conway Twitty, Hank Williams and some banjo picking guys who sang with an exaggerated southern drawl. Mom, riding shotgun, would be talking non-stop over all this drama.

"What a beautiful landscape! Look at that barn! What do you want for dinner? Do we have any pop? What kind? I made sandwiches--they're in the cooler! What are you reading? What books did you bring with you? Oh, look! Ice cream!"

Mom didn't expect responses to any of her questions, which was good as most of the time nobody could follow the tangents closely enough to answer. Sometimes the constant commentary annoyed me, interfering as it did with the further adventures of the Hardy Boys or Alfred Hitchcock and the Three Investigators, but most of the time, I enjoyed it. Mom could always be counted on to be clutching a guidebook and spouting off facts about history, the path of this highway, or the legends surrounding such-and-such a landmark, or, god forbid we come within a hundred miles of a scenic turn-off. Back in those days, scenic turn-offs were snatched up with more fervor than a new iPhone application. Travel and Mom were synonymous to me and her eagerness to learn everything about the place you were going to visit stayed with me for life.

Many years later, Dad traded the station wagon in on a newer model. He kept Mom.

RELATED TANGENT #3
Journal Entry from Friday, June 2009
It's 9:02 in the morning on a hot, midwestern July Tuesday in the year 2009 and I'm sitting in a coffee shop in Iowa City looking at a

picture of my birth family. I've been staring at this picture, trying to write about the significance it has for me and failing miserably. It's a simple picture, really, so it shouldn't be this difficult to write about, although this is the first time I've ever looked at this picture so closely before. It's a wallet-sized shot of four people: me, my sister Nan, Mom and Dad. I remember this photo was taken several years ago at the Walmart in Tennessee during a visit to my parents. Mom and Dad sit next to each other, with Mom on Dad's right. She is wearing a green sweater, dangling earrings and a tasteful necklace. Dad wears a short sleeved pink shirt which Mom always said was salmon but--let's face it--it's pink. What the hell is this with "salmon" anyway? A grey sweater vest covers Dad's salmon-colored shirt. My sister stands behind Mom and I loom behind my father with my hand on his shoulder. I am shocked and embarrassed to see that my face and balding head practically reflect the light like aluminum foil. I'm surprised the photographer didn't need shades. I want to blame this on poor lighting, lack of gels, or perhaps a bad filter on the camera. But I know that it is more than likely my own fault--I hate the sun and avoid it at all costs, the effect of which makes me look like a human-sized Pillsbury Doughboy. My sister's the only one with tan skin, but she also buys a lot of Avon, so it's probably a tan from a tube.

Trying to write about the history of the photo, I remember how annoying that day was Nan's three kids came along to get "family photos" of her family as well as a shot of Mom, Dad, her and me. I thought it was a totally asinine idea, as my brother-in-law was out of town doing god-knows what for the rich oil company that weekend and why the hell should we go to Walmart for family photos when we could just as easily take them with Mom's digital camera? I mean, her husband wasn't there, so how could it be a "family photo" when the father is absent? I told my sister that it would either make people think we were one of those trashy Jerry Springer type "absentee father" families or just plain mean to her husband who isn't such a bad guy despite the fact he's a Bush-loving Republican. She told me to stop being such a politically correct fag and take the damn picture or else I couldn't borrow her convertible anymore and have to take the gas-guzzling SUV that sucks through tons of gas--that only she *and my brother-in-law can afford because he gets a discount on his gas. She knew it would piss me off to fork over that much money to big business, so I shut up.*

I'm surprised to see both Mom and Dad are wearing their glasses. I remember asking Dad on the way to Walmart if he wanted me to drive and he answered that if I drive, I'd give him a heart attack because I drive like a mad man and if I wanted to drive myself into a cliff, go ahead, but don't take anyone else with me. His eyes twinkled when he said this, which is how I knew he was teasing. His sarcasm was often derailed by that twinkle. Many people who didn't know him often mistook good natured ribbing for meanness. Hell, I did, too, for the first thirty-five years of my life. It was only after I realized my own smart-assed quips were sired by his sarcasm that I learned how to deal with it. I didn't take the driving comment too seriously, though, as Dad was . . . well . . . Dad: he had to be in control of anything with a motor.

I'm wearing that blue shirt mom got for me from the second-hand store. (At first glance, I mistook it for the one I bought at the dollar store, but thankfully it is not. It would depress me to know that my last photo taken with my father was in a shirt from the Dollar Store on Highway 70 in Sparta, Tennessee. In true redneck fashion, it's not sophisticated enough to be a Dollar Store; it's a Dollar Mart or some such place. On that visit, I got a shirt for $2.99. I remember the price because I didn't want to pay $2.99 in a Dollar Store. It should be a Dollar Store because things cost a dollar. If they were going to charge $2.99, then it should be called the $2.99 Store.)

I woke up on the morning this picture was taken to Dad announcing that the family was going to Wally World, home of the sweat-shop-human-rights-abusers and we needed to get dressed for pictures. I pitched a fit.

"Thanks, Dad," I remember snapping. "All I've got is frickin' t-shirts. Why didn't you tell me before I left Seattle?"

"Because then you'd have nothing to bitch about. Now get your ass in gear."

"You hate getting your picture taken." I reminded him.

His answer mystified me. "We haven't had a family picture in years and I want a family picture." I remember asking Mom if he had taken his blood pressure medication because he was acting funny and Mom rolled her eyes.

"I have no idea, but if he doesn't get this god-damned picture, he's going to drive me up a frickin' wall. Just go put on one of those shirts I got for you at the second-hand store and take the picture so we can get it over with."

I flung open the closet of the guest bedroom with trepidation. My mom is all the time buying clothes for people, it's a curse, I think, as the poor woman is often times found wandering the aisles of a store, spinning in circles trying to find a pair of pants, shirt or other article of clothing that a family member would like. It's her talisman against bad shopping karma: as long as she leaves a place with SOMETHING for SOMEONE, she is sure to find a great bargain for herself. God forbid there's a sale. The basement is crammed full of Christmas wrapping paper, bows, boxes and trinkets that she hauled home on December 26th with the battle cry, "IT WAS ON SALE!"

To my surprise, the shirts were classy numbers that looked good on me.

"They should look good on you," she told me. "I got these from a second hand store that got them from a very wealthy lawyer in Florida. Lawyers always have great clothes."

"Why did he give them up?" I asked.

"I don't know. He didn't want them, he retired, he died. Who knows?"

So I found myself headed to take a family portrait wearing a shirt that probably belonged to a dead lawyer. Shakespeare would be proud.

Between Dad's insistence on taking a picture, my sister defending Walmart, the sweat-shop-human-rights-abusers and my annoyance with the whole thing, I'm surprised we made it through the day.

The picture didn't turn out half bad, though, despite the tacky fabric background that was supposed to reflect tasteful splotches of color but instead looked like an Iowa thunderstorm before the tornado wipes out the fields.

There were several pictures of the family taken that day and this is only one of the poses. Several more were taken of my sister and her three kids who behaved like total spoiled brats until I threatened *to smack the shit out of them. When my sister said, "Fine, go ahead." They finally started to behave.*

Sitting here right now looking at the two photos, I realize this is the only one where Dad is <u>almost</u> smiling. He has never smiled in pictures as far back as I can remember. I'm not sure why.

I find myself obsessing on this picture and I just figured out why: Dad was so insistent about the family doing this photo shoot and, as fate would dictate, it is the last portrait he took before his heart attack. Why would a man who hated having his picture taken be so determined to get a family photo? If he was so intent on getting a family picture, why didn't we all gather in the back yard near the lake and snap a couple shots? Instead, he got an appointment, trucked on down to Wally World and forced us to sit against a phony sunset backdrop while children and old ladies screamed in the background. Mom and I often wondered if Dad knew that he would be dead within the year.

PART TWO: EUROPE
May, 2000: Brussels, Belgium
Before the E.U. Currency

The new millennia may have marked the year of "Y2K" to the rest of the world, but in my corner of the universe only two milestones existed: getting my Master's degree and (finally) getting to see Europe. As much as I love learning, enduring the two years in grad school felt just slightly easier than enduring an evening of watching *Glitter* on an endless loop. I stood on the edge of graduation like a guy skydiving: the journey ahead holds nothing but a downhill slide, but it's better than standing still. Not to mention there's only so much of the usual grad school slavery one can do before your head explodes; the papers, the volumes of reading, the grading papers handed in by freshmen who can barely find their dorms much less a reference book, and the politics of the average Master's committee. (Note for those considering graduate school: Your grade is directly proportional to your expertise in ass-kissing.) To compound this, I had a culture clash to contend with. I'm from Chicago, lived in Los Angeles and Seattle--the southern way of life was as alien as another dimension. The first time someone asked me, "Are you cold?" I answered that, no, I wasn't. Only later did my kind-hearted boss teach me Southern lingo: south of the Mason-Dixon line "Are you cold?" means "I'm cold. Can I shut the window?" Who knew?

I needed out of the apartment, out of the city, out of the rat race. I needed a celebration. How did I make it to thirty-seven without seeing Europe? I was a theatre major, for crying out loud! Why weren't tours of The Globe and London's West End a course requirement?

When I suggested to Mom that she accompany me, my then-boyfriend and his sister on this trip, she lit up like a Christmas tree. I wish I could take credit for the idea of asking Mom, but, as usual, it sort of happened. My father listened patiently to my excited description of the upcoming trip and then ceased his usual bitching and moaning about traveling abroad by surprising me with saying, "You should take your mother with you."

"You should be the one to go to Europe with her, Dad, not me," I said. It was a taunt, I suppose, as I knew fully well that his first trip overseas was the AAA-approved love child of a nightmare and torture. Just bringing up the idea probably caused him to break out in hives.

"Like hell!" he said, swinging the remote around to watch ESPN on the biggest large-screen TV I had ever seen in my life. "I wouldn't go back to that place if you paid me."

"I don't know, Dad . . ."

"Well, if you don't want to . . . don't . . ."

"It's not that--"

He glared at me while I floundered. "You can show her around all the sights. She'd like that."

I watched him fondle the TV remote and shift his recliner into third gear; the gear of SLEEP. A thought suddenly struck me--he wants me to take her because he couldn't. He had come to accept the fact that while he may physically be able to trundle up and down European cities, his own psyche prevented him from doing it. He knew that he could never bring his wife back to the place to which she wanted to return, so by getting me to take Mom, he would be giving her the gift of Europe while never leaving the comfort of his recliner. He was asking me to be his surrogate.

"I think that would be fun to take Mom. Do you think she'd go if I asked her to?"

He snorted. "She's probably already packed."

Ironically, Dad turned out to be the one who, later, almost killed the excursion. The plan was almost identical to the plan Mom and I devised a few years ago when she went with me to New York: Mom would fly out of Nashville, we would rendezvous at JFK, board a plane for London and for the next two weeks, throw caution to the wind and hurl ourselves through Europe with all the abandon of wayward teenagers.

For thirty-seven years I have avoided going on vacation with a group of people out of fear of being stuck in a tour group. I know myself--I would hover over my travel companions with the codependent fervor of Julie the Cruise Director. We would all be responsible for our own expenses, thereby alleviating the fear of getting stiffed with the check at some five-star European restaurant. After we discussed the ground rules, Mom eagerly accepted. It was Dad who balked.

"You're going to go all the way overseas without any hotel reservations?" he grumbled, digging into the Sunday football snacks Mom prepared for him. "She's not eighteen years old, she needs a bed to sleep in and a place to sit down once in a while. She's going to get hurt in some God-damned backward country."

"Dad, we've got to follow our hearts . . . go where the spirit takes us . . . let the universe guide us. It's going to be an adventure!" That was during my "free spirit" phase when the idea of becoming stranded in some remote city on another continent was artistic and bohemian. NOTE TO SELF: The difference between thirty-seven and forty-seven--common sense.

"It's going to be a disaster! That's the most ridiculous thing I've ever heard!" he spouted. "How can you go to a foreign country and not even know where you're staying?"

I tuned him out for a few minutes while he rattled on about how I would wind up getting my mother arrested, how communist-loving Europeans love to prey on naive Americans, how he heard from a friend-of-a-friend that a second cousin twice removed was abducted by fiendish Scandinavians--the usual overprotective spousal issues. I don't blame him, really. He never forgave me for the New York sex shop fiasco. Add to that his own negative experience oversees and his belief that any place where you can travel for an hour without seeing a McDonald's is primitive, I can see where Europe may be more frightening than Freddy Kruger. Besides, I'm the template for Scarlett O'Hara. I tend to be irresponsible and lack the DNA that predisposes one to plan . . . anything . . . I don't read emails thoroughly, I leap before I look and worry about things tomorrow. In his shoes, I wouldn't let my cat go on a vacation with me.

Spurred on by both the self-imposed expectation that Mom should have a good time and Dad's insistence that Mom avoid living on the street for three weeks (apparently she's not cut out to be a Bohemian), I promised Dad that I would secure a place to stay on three nights; the two nights following our arrival in London and the night in Germany before she headed back to the states. Thanks to a website specializing in low-cost vacations, I arranged to rent some guy's apartment for three days.

"What about the rest of the time?" Dad asked, picking at his pork rinds.

"I gave you three days!"

"You want to stay for three Goddamn weeks!"

"We'll take it as it comes, Dad," I assured him, "I don't want to be tied to schedules."

"That's bullshit!" He spat. "What if you can't find a place to stay?"

"Dad, Europe is a big place that's older than the United States. I'm sure someone, someplace is going to have a hotel room with running water."

"Yeah, at some dive, or some opium den." Dad's voice was hitting a higher octave, so I knew this was important to him. I may be taking my mom, but she was his wife.

"Don't worry about it," Mom assured Dad. "It'll be fun. I'm easy. I ain't cheap, but I'm easy!"

"I'm trusting you that you won't let anything happen to her," Dad's face hardened as he pointed his finger at me.

"You worry too much," I laughed at him. "What's the worst that can happen?"

"That's what you said about New York and she wound up in a sex shop!"

I wanted to remind him that a gay sex shop was one of the safest places for a mother to be, but I held my tongue. Fathers didn't carry the political sway with homos like mothers did. Besides, he was shooting me the Dad Look.

***

The night our train rolled into Brussels, the rain poured down so thick and heavy that we suspected the residents were two steps away from building an ark. The then-boyfriend, his sister and I grabbed our convenient, easily-stowed-in-an-overhead-compartment roller bags and breezed off the economy class sleeper car, while Mom hauled her behemoth dufflebag out of the bowels of the train. I stood on the platform and shook my head while she wrestled with oversized monstrosity. I had purchased a large backpack-style travel bag with sturdy, reinforced frame and wheels. I knew Mom couldn't throw something like that on her back, but she could wheel it around. I offered to buy her one, but she convinced me she had it under control. But when I got off the plane at Heathrow, I knew we were in trouble when we stood by the carousel in the baggage claim area and she said, "Just lift it off of the carousel conveyor belt for me. I can roll it from there. It's not too heavy." After which, I nearly gave myself a hernia yanking the thing over the lip of the baggage carousel. The following three days were spent convincing Mom she needed to get a new piece of luggage. I kept hoping she was going to get in touch with her inner Bohemian, throw her underwear to the wind and downsize to a fits-easily-into-the-overhead-bin kind of travel case, to no avail. What she selected was a dufflebag with wheels. While it was still smaller than her previous leviathan, it still looked large enough to hide Jimmy Hoffa and his cement shoes. For weeks prior to leaving America, I pleaded with her to pack light. She assured me she was.

"I'm bringing old underwear, so as they get dirty, I can throw them away."

"That's not packing light. That's UN-packing light."

"They don't weigh anything."

"Tell me what you have." For the next six minutes, I listened to the litany of items that constituted "packing light" for my mother: namely everything in the bathroom except the toilet paper.

"Don't you think that's packing light?" she asked.

"No, Ma, I don't," I told her. "To begin with, you can't use a blow dryer in Europe without some funny connection doo-hickey. They have 220 electricity and we have 110."

"Oh, that's right," Mom said. "I knew that. I ran into that problem in Italy visiting your sister. I'll bring the connector."

"No! Ma! Dump the blow dryer."

"But the blow dryer doesn't weigh anything!"

"How about the shoes?"

"I can't go everywhere in the same shoes! Besides, they don't weigh anything."

"Tell you what: I plan on doing laundry along the way, because I'm only bringing clothes for four days. Take less. We can do laundry together."

"That's a great idea!" she said. "We can use the time to bond."

I thought our discussions had cinched it. Oversized, overweight dufflebag full of stuff she'll never use: 1. Son: 0.

Brussels was my first European train station and I exited the Eurostar with a giddy sense of excitement. In movies, all European train stations seem perversely romantic, full of acute shadows and wayward corners for clandestine meetings. Brussels: not so much. What greeted me was a tattered building with fading paint, dirty windows and the overpowering smell of urine. Urine is a popular smell in Europe. Maybe its the throngs of people practically living on top of each other; maybe it's the lack of bathrooms (although by now we've learned that there's money to be made in them there loo visits), or maybe Europeans don't harbor the aversion to bodily fluids like Americans and don't mind pissing in alleys. I never discovered the answer to this perplexing question, so I prefer to remember the smell not as "stale body waste", but as a harbinger of good fortune; as if the Powers That Be were purposely leaving puddles of piss to mark us as their chosen ones. We were the visitors to God's dog park.

We hauled our bags outside into the night. Storm clouds blotted out what stars hang out over the Belgian sky. I'm sure the Europeans can name the constellations visible in their night sky . . . but let's face it, I'm American. I have an iPhone with a constellation app. The wind blew lightly across the city, picking up speed and dropping the temperature, so by the time it blew across us, the chill eradicated the remnants of grogginess that had set in during the train ride from Brugge. We had exited at the main entrance to the station and stood on a cracked cement sidewalk paralleling a vacant, dark street, surrounded by wet pedestrians and dim street lamps. By European standards it was a street, but by U.S. standards the four feet wide ribbon of pavement barely qualified as an alley.

"Well, we're here," Mom asked. "What now?"

"Well . . . we walk to the hostel."

"How far is it?"

"Haven't a clue."

"Yeah, right," Mom sounded less than thrilled.

I shrugged. "I'm sure we can find it."

"I don't think so."

Ever since I moved to Seattle, rain has never been a deterrent for me. The first joke I learned about the Pacific Northwest is, "What do you call a Seattleite with an umbrella? A tourist." It rains here. A lot. Days can pass without seeing the sun. Which is exactly why I enjoy living here, as I am more apt to walk in the rain than walk in the sun. Rain gets you wet. Sun gets you skin cancer. You can live with wet clothes. Living without epidermis is a bit trickier.

In the end, Mom and I decided to hail a cab. The driver spoke no English, but, thankfully, could read. We presented him with the printout of the website for our hostel, nodded and motioned for us to get into the car. I hauled Mom's dufflebag to the rear of the vehicle, thinking I was being kind to the driver, an offer to help load the bag into the trunk. As I approached the rear, I heard a soft "click" and the trunk popped open. The driver made no move to get out of the car. Perhaps it was the rain. He was middle eastern and middle-easterners are like Southern Californians--they melt in water like the Wicked Witch of the West. After the four of us squeezed into the vehicle, we took off into the darkness with the same gusto as a Manhattan cabbie on speed. The task of calculating the exchange rate fell to me, as I was the unlucky sod with the mother who loves to give people gadgets as gifts. Just before we left the states, Mom presented me with her latest find; a thin calculator device that came in a box along with a very thick instruction book.

"What is it?" I asked, unwrapping the surprise gift.

"A portable dictionary and exchange rate calculator!" Mom's enthusiasm knew no bounds.

"How do I use it?"

"Read the manual, dummy."

I held up the thick book and began thumbing through it. "The instructions are thicker than the gadget."

"You'll figure it out."

It took me about an hour to figure out how to turn it on, a day to figure out how to change from DICTIONARY to CURRENCY

EXCHANGE and a week to understand how to plug in the formula. With the thrill of a man who just scaled Mount Everest, I called her giddy with glee.

"I did it!" I bragged.

"Good. You can take care of the money," Mom said. "Then if I come home broke, I can blame you."

No sweat. I had it together. Or rather I THOUGHT I did until we sat on a train somewhere outside of Brugge. We seem to have burned through the British pounds with amazing speed and I had a strange suspicion that my electronic mastery hadn't been quite so mastered. Grabbing my reading glasses, I poured through the instruction book again--this time, unhampered by phones, emails and other people to talk to. Thus far on our trip, I had assumed that the value of the U.S. dollar was input first, then the exchange rate; the resulting number would be the local equivalent, which we then could calculate into Euros without the aid of technology. But when the calculator came back with some astronomically ridiculous number, I gave up and handed it off to Mom, who tossed it back to me like some twentieth-century hot potato. Between us, we were able to figure out that we had just spent a week in London giving everyone double the tip we intended. Great . . . first they forced Margaret Thatcher upon us, then they used us to double their Gross Domestic Product. The U.K. SO owed us one.

The cab screeched to a halt in front of a narrow brick building standing between what appeared to be two vacant warehouses. The driver nodded to us, then to the building. It didn't take an Einstein to interpret the body language: we had arrived. As the cab idled, and rain poured down in sheets on a night so black I couldn't see my hand in front of my face, I bent down in front of the cab's headlights so I could see inside my wallet. Suddenly remembering that I had neglected to calculate the exchange rate, I gave him $40 American. I figured if it wasn't enough he'd spit on me or whatever it was Belgian people do when insulted. When his face lit up and he started nodding saying, "Danke! Thanks to you! Gracias!" I knew I figured I had just given him a 1,000% tip. Nobody says "Thank you" in three languages, not even a cab driver.

As our two traveling companions had evaporated into thin air, Mom and I were left to check into the hostel. Luckily, the young workers knew some English and spoke it clearly enough to inform us that yes, they DO rent linens. This was when I learned that, in "Hostel Terms" linens are what we Americans call "sheets". Mom asked about towels and the workers rolled their eyes.

"No. No towels. Linens."

"Aren't towels 'linens'?" Mom whispered to me.

"Not in Brussels." I told her.

"We didn't bring towels?" Mom asked.

"Not me."

"How are we going to shower?" She asked.

"Showering isn't the problem. It's the drying off part that is tricky." I found it hard to believe that tucked away in a duffle bag the size of a woolly mammoth Mom didn't have a towel. My mother is the kind who carries one of everything in her purse "just in case". I think she watched too much TV in the '70s and was lead to believe that at any minute the producers of *Let's Make a Deal* would snatch her off the street and offer her a million bucks for a 1957 penny. How a woman who straps hand sanitizer to her purse would go to Europe without a towel mystified me. I knew why I didn't--I'm impulsive and reckless. But Mom? Unbelievable.

More surprises awaited us upstairs in the room.

"I thought you said we had a bath?" Mom asked.

"I did." I looked at the 10X10 room. It was utilitarian and clean: a white tiled floor, large window overlooking a dark street, two sets of bunk beds and a sink.

"Where's the bathroom?" Mom asked

How was I supposed to know that in Hostel Language, a "bath" means a sink? Apparently, showers aren't foremost in most European's minds. Positive that somewhere a shower and toilet were hidden away from the crazed masses of smelly travelers, Mom headed into the hallway with one mission: find the shower. A moment later she returned, a frown on her face. "There's one bathroom for the whole floor," she said shaking her head. "The toilet and the shower are over there." She pointed across the hallway. "No towels."

One of the fun rituals of traveling is investigating the hotel room when you arrive at in a new city. Although the rooms vary little from place to place, I find it impossible to resist the temptation to look under the bed, open the drawers and click through the TV stations. This is a childish ritual, as most of the time you find nothing but lint, a Gideon Bible and pay-per-view porn, but I do it nonetheless. One time I found a stash of condoms under the bed and a couple of matchbooks in the drawer. I suppose I should have been repulsed by the lack-luster maid service, but I thought it was funny. Kind of like a scavenger hunt without the running around town inviting disaster.

So while the ex and his sister headed out to find a store for snacks and, if possible, some towels, Mom and I explored the room. Three minutes later we sat on the bunk beds looking at each other expectantly. (NOTE TO SELF: the difference between HOTEL ROOM and HOSTEL is one dresser and no bathroom.)

"What do we do now?" she asked. I shrugged. There wasn't a TV to watch, nor a comfy chair to curl up in and read a book. So far, hostels in Brussels were a bust.

Mom opened up her mammoth duffle bag, reached in and handed me a small package wrapped in cellophane. I ripped open the cellophane to reveal a tiny hand-towel brilliantly colored with embroidered red, blue and gold sea life. Along one side was a scene of a cartoon fish underwater billowing cute cartoon air bubbles and on the opposite side, seaweed. It was adorable. It was dry. It was about four inches square.

"It gets bigger when it gets wet."

"I hope so." I said, holding up the Barbie sized towel.

"Try it and see."

"Where? For what?"

"In the sink." She motioned to the corner. "I saw them in the store and thought they were cute. I got myself one, too." She pulled another fabric sample from her bag. "They were on sale!"

"What do we use them for, Mom?" Even if they did grow when they got wet, they'd only dry off a person the size of Mini-Me.

"Oh, I don't know," she said, opening her towel and admiring it. "But I got them two for a dollar."

Shortly after our discovery of the mini-towels, our traveling companions arrived from the store with cigarettes, snacks and couple of rolls of paper towels. Mom grabbed a role of paper towels and shrugged.

"What the hell. I'll pretend we're camping," she said, heading across the hall to the communal bathroom.

While the other two unpacked, the movie theatre in my mind ran COMING ATTRACTIONS of Dad's tantrum when he found out about this leg of the journey. We hadn't been across the Atlantic for a week and already we'd forced Mom to violate the one cardinal rule she had laid out for us before leaving the States: she didn't want to share a bathroom.

In the end, we all learned a couple valuable lessons: it only takes a half roll of paper towels to dry off after a shower; it pays to clarify "bathroom" and "shower" when reserving rooms at a hostel; and those tiny travel towels really do get bigger when they get wet.

"Told you so," Mom said proudly. "Aren't you happy I bought them?" she asked after I had showered that night. "Now what do you think about your crazy mother?"

I shrugged and held up the fabric, which had expanded to the size of a kitchen dish towel. "Who knew?"

"Trust your mother," She said, climbing into the bottom bunk. "Now you have to convince your father that I'm doing fine not staying in expensive hotels. I'm easy. I ain't cheap, but I'm easy."

"Dad is never to find out about this," I said. "He's already got one strike against me for reserving a hostel instead of a Hilton. If he finds out about the shared bathroom, he'll kill me."

"Oh, there's plenty of other things for him to kill you for." she said, settling in.

Great, I thought. There's still two weeks left. Maybe with luck I'll be kidnapped by a band of Gypsies, face an ancient Belgian curse, or carried off by a crazed Pterodactyl. The Gypsies would be preferable. I look pretty good in loose-fitting clothes.

***

When we checked in last night, the two college coeds pretending to be front desk clerks informed us that the hostel provided "light food to break the fast". Their misuse of English was cute: What they lacked in proficiency they made up for in enthusiasm. We assumed "light food" didn't mean air-puffed junk food like marshmallows and Cheetoes, so the next morning we threw on our still-wet clothing and cursed the lack of an in-room coffee maker. Hostels are cheap accommodations geared to young folks who think sleeping in a sheep pasture during a rain storm is quaint, so I didn't worry about showering before heading down to break my fast. I just shoved a baseball cap on my head and headed out the door. I felt a bit nervous over being the oldest one in the room. Mom, on the other hand, didn't care.

"I'm old," she told me with a shrug. "Get over it." While she didn't look her fifty-plus years, she certainly didn't look twenty either. We descended the stairs to the common room where the continental breakfast lay spread out like a days-old salad bar at Sizzler.

To my surprise, the crowd in the huge dining area was anything but college-aged kids. The people gobbling cheese and gnawing on toast ranged from the very young to couples that looked to be approximately Mom's age.

"I guess it's not just college kids," I said to Mom.

"Thank god. That's all we need--kegger parties and loud music all night."

"Ma," I said, "You have insomnia anyway."

"I know. I'm just jealous they're having more fun than I am."

I wanted to ask how she knew about kegger parties, but was afraid of the answer I may hear. A woman who blunders into a Greenwich Village sex shop certainly won't let a keg of beer and puking college kids stop her.

We took our place in line and moved slowly past the yogurt, cereal and fresh fruit.

"I wonder if I can order eggs." Mom asked.

"You can ask," I shrugged.

"Ah, never mind, it's okay. I'm easy. I ain't cheap, but I'm easy."

Unlike the United States, where sugar or corn syrup is mated with chemicals, then added to everything, food in Europe contains vitamins and nutrients. All my friends had warned me not to expect the sugary sweetness of the states, but I didn't realize how serious they were until the morning after our arrival in Europe last week. We had just sat down to our first breakfast in Great Britain. I glanced around the table, unable to identify any of the foodstuffs set out by our host. I honed in on the small plastic yogurt containers. Ah! The familiar pictures of berries and honey I had come to know and love! I ripped open the lid and dug in. The bitter, tongue-curling tartness ripped at my taste buds and set my mouth watering. If this was natural food, I wanted my corn syrup back. Sure it packs on the gelatinous fat, but I'm an American. We like sweet-tasting goodies. Gelatinous fat is what Weight Watchers was invented for.

So when Mom wondered about her eggs, I secretly hoped she'd succeed in finding a chicken. The thought of another breakfast of cold cereal with the taste and texture of cardboard made me want to hurl bangers and mash at the nearest Brit. I meandered over to the table housing the hot foods and my eyes fell upon the Holy Grail of breakfast glory: scrambled eggs mixed with bacon bits. I motioned for Mom to come over.

"Grab us some!" She said, pushing me to the table.

Clutching a plate, I made my way through the throng surrounding the hotplates and elbowed into position. I watched as spoonful after spoonful of eggs disappeared onto the plates of the other guests, who apparently hadn't eaten in days, judging by the way they piled on the food.

Just as I approached the hotplate, an arm appeared from the other side of the table. It belonged to a husky man with several gold chains around his neck and a thick Rolex watch. I looked at him in disappointment as he spooned out the rest of the scrambled eggs and handed me the spoon before turning to disappear into the crowd. Just then I spotted a hostel worker approaching with a huge stack of toast. I motioned to the empty bowl and he shrugged.

"Eggs gone."

I returned to Mom bearing an orange.

"That's okay. I like oranges. I'm easy. I ain't cheap, but I'm easy," she said.

***

With every step, I felt the echo reverberate through my intestines. My stomach churned and growled so loudly people mistook me for a crazed coyote. We had been hiking through Brussels all day, totally skipping lunch and when I suggested an early dinner, everyone agreed. Mom kept saying, "I'm easy. I ain't cheap, but I'm easy," and by now I was ready to toss her into the street, because she proved this to be a lie; every time I tried to duck into a restaurant along the way, Mom shook her head no. It was her opinion that we had already eaten something similar yesterday, or the menu didn't look good, or the place looked old and dirty.

"Mom," I explained, trying to keep from yelling, "this is Europe. Everything's old."

"Old, yes, but not dirty."

"You need to cut them some slack," I said. "These buildings survived World War Two for God's sake."

"From the looks of them, so did the food."

I looked around, praying to spot something familiar amongst all the neon. I didn't bring my travel dictionary and, thus, couldn't read the street signs, so I could have died from hunger two blocks from a Pizza Hut. I wanted food. I didn't care about the ethnicity, the price, or the cleanliness of the building's exterior. My head felt helium-filled and my knees buckled. I was well on my way to joining the Donner Party and Hannibal Lector as "People You Don't Want To Have Dinner With". How in the hell did this happen? It's Europe, for God's sake, not the Sahara. It's not like we were stranded in miles of sand looking for an oasis. We've been passing Burger Kings, McDonald's and take-away Teriyaki places for blocks.

Despite the attack of restaurant indecisiveness and possible foray into cannibalism, I had the sense to marvel at how lucky we were to be here. Although I didn't know it at the time, Mom and I had come to Europe at the perfect time. The whole world seemed to be riding high on the prosperity and sense of frivolity that accompanied Clinton's administration. It was during those fun years when American tourists still traveled abroad with a sense of adventure and were usually met with polite warmth. The U.S. had yet to experience the horrifying events of 9-11, The Department of Homeland Security or George W. Bush.

Just as Mom and I debated the priorities of our next culinary exploration of the day (she demanded cleanliness; I demanded the ability to serve something edible that didn't have its head and feet still attached), we happened to pass a magnificent brick building flashing a host of neon lights advertising an array of international beers and alcohols. Several people in long coats and wide brimmed hats sat beneath a thick fog of cigarette smoke at small metal cafe tables which lined the sidewalk, looking like anemic aliens under the phosphorescent lights. In unison, we turned and strode through the front door without a word being spoken--four empty stomachs turning into crazed tourists on the hunt for french fries.

In the states, we'd call this place a sports pub. In the center of the cavernous, dimly lit room, a long, wide wooden bar dwarfed everything and everybody. Surrounding it in ever-widening circles were heavy wooden tables. In the far corner, easily visible from the bar, was a large-screen TV. A dozen college students sat at the tables poring over notebooks, clutching a highlighter or a pint of beer. Open text books lay stacked around them like paper fortresses, while pens, rulers and cigarette lighters rolled freely amongst the chaos. We took a seat at a round wooden table all the way at the back, behind the bar and next to the kitchen, where the aroma of grilling burgers teased me.

Within minutes, a beautiful young blonde woman walked up to the table, laid down four menus and whipped out an order pad. She asked us something, but since I didn't speak the language, I had no idea what she said. Assuming the European wait staff operated the same as American wait staff, I jumped to the conclusion we were supposed to tell her what we wanted to drink.

I mimed drinking and said, "Water."

"Do you speak English?" Mom asked. I shot her a venomous glance. "What?"

"You can't assume everyone speaks English."

"You never know unless you ask!" Mom snapped.

The woman's eyes lit up and a huge smile spread across her face. "English? Yes. I am to learn English in the college." Her voice was breathy and the final words of her sentences went up at the end, so everything she said lilted like an exam question.

"See? I told you," Mom chastised me. Then to the waitress said, "What are the specials?"

The woman stared at Mom for a second, her eyebrows wrinkling as she processed this. Then, with a sharp intake of breath she responded with exuberance. "The special food?"

She rattled off a couple dishes starring German sausage and featuring enough cholesterol to stop a heart at twenty paces. I loved her airy, breathy voice that tinkled with excitement. Her English came out in spurts, as if her brain processed each phrase as a separate unit. The verb tenses were haphazard, the accents on the wrong syllables and she said too many "the"s, but she did have a wonderful grasp of English. When she left to place the food order, Mom nudged me.

"Most of the Europeans can speak English now."

"Yeah, but we should TRY to speak their language. It's only polite."

Mom thought about this and nodded. "Yes, we should. But either we learn the language in five minutes so we can order, or they speak English. I thought you were hungry."

"You are so typical American." I scolded.

"Yes, I am," Mom nodded. "And there's nothing wrong with being American."

I wanted to argue with her--to accuse her of having the same arrogant American attitude that so many from the States bring with them when they travel in Europe. In the end, hunger won out. Political correctness dies in the face of a German sausage.

"Besides, they probably want to practice speaking English."

"They do not want to practice," I grumbled, hoping the breathy blonde remembered to bring us some bread.

The woman returned with our drinks and a couple baskets of bread. As she paused, her face contorted in deep thought, I dug into the loaf like a starving character from a bad post-apocalyptic movie. My mouth was crammed full of sourdough when she burst out with, "I would like to practice English. May I speak it with you?" She was so cute. I wanted to wrap her up and take her home, but I was too busy chewing.

"Told you," Mom muttered under her breath.

Damn, I hate it when she's right.

"How long have you been learning English?" Mom asked. Being a terminal student, I have frequently been asked to chat with people so they can practice their English, but they never suggest a subject. Usually, my English practice sessions deteriorate into a stilted interview with all the interest of watching the city council chambers on closed-circuit television.

"Oh, long time. I started learning the English in the small school . . . school for the young."

"Elementary school? Primary school? Grade school?" Mom tapped my shoulder and motioned for me to add more ideas. What was this? *The Million Dollar Pyramid*? Suddenly the woman nodded furiously.

"I not practice much. And when I do, I do not know if I speak the English properly."

"You're doing fine," Mom encouraged. "So you're in college now?"

Before I knew it, our waitress had told us all about her school experiences, her desire to speak fluently "like an American" and, finally, her Big Dream; she was determined to visit the one place she had longed to see: Florida. She wanted to see alligators in the everglades, Mickey Mouse in the Magic Kingdom, and the sandy beaches of the gulf coast. Her face lit up when she spoke of Florida with all the glowing warmth of a woman gazing upon her first born child.

"Florida's a horrible place," I said. "It's hot. Humid. Too many tourists."

"How about Chicago?" Mom suggested. "That's where we're from." She announced proudly.

She cringed. "I want to see the beautiful beaches of Miami. I want to visit the sunny, sandy beaches."

"Sandy beaches hiding the used heroin needles," I muttered to Mom.

"Chicago's much better," I said to the woman.

"Too many guns," she said, shaking her head.

"Well, if that's what you want to do," Mom said, "good luck. Eat an orange."

As she left to check on our order, Mom turned to me. "Guns? Is she kidding me?"

"She's going to be so disappointed when she sees Florida."

"Maybe she's never seen a beach," Mom suggested. "She doesn't know the fish should be IN the water, not floating around on top of it."

I noticed our waitress chatting with a group of college students near the kitchen, but thought nothing of it until a few minutes later when she showed up at the table with a tray and a couple of the young people in tow.

"They are learning the English, too," she motioned to the new faces. "I want you to have this. Thank you for helping me speak the English," placing a plate of appetizers on the table.

"You want to practice your English, too?" I asked the pack of students, trying to sound upbeat. They looked sweet, but we had been out all day sight-seeing and I was tired.

"The more the merrier!" Mom said, her voice booming with excitement. Before the students could settle themselves into the chairs they dragged from surrounding tables, Mom was firing questions at them: Where they were from? What they were studying in school? Was English hard to learn? I'm not sure if she wanted to help them with their English as much as she wanted to chat with someone else besides the three of us. Sure, I'm her son, but there's only so much family one can take before the idea of EMPTY NEST SYNDROME becomes a fantasy.

Throughout the next few hours, we collected a cluster of young people, all eager to talk to us using the English. After about an hour, I felt myself becoming short tempered. I enjoyed the opportunity to chat with the locals, but I really wanted to head back to the room. Mom seemed to be having the time of her life, though. She nodded furiously whenever their broken English made sense, or they correctly used an idiom. When the communication broke down, she gesticulated wildly--a mutant compilation of mime and yelling--as if the arm movements would improve their English skills. Her conversation flowed freely and her patience endless. I thought about what I would say to Dad when she told him about her foray into becoming a language model--which she would, as she told him everything that happened with meticulous detail Anderson Cooper would envy. Is this the kind of harmless interchange he would find charming? Or would he add "chatting with strange Belgian students" to the list of DANGEROUS ENCOUNTERS beneath "New York sex shop"?

As the conversation began to wind down, I mimed to the waitress to bring the check. She helped me count out the local currency and took the money with great flourish. I didn't know how much to tip, though.

"Tip?" She looked at me through squinted eyes.

"Yes, extra money for you, to say 'thank you' for good service."

She shrugged. "It is up to you, but none is required." She must have noticed the odd look on my face, for she laughed politely and continued. "You do this tip in America. In my country, all jobs pay enough. We do work we love, not for money. If you do a job you love, life is better."

I wrote those words down in my journal. I think they're onto something, those crazy Europeans. They commit themselves to employment because it is something they enjoy, not because it pays enough to buy an SUV. In Brussels at least, "work" isn't a four letter word.

Sometime after the check was paid, but before the students ordered their last beer, Mom had picked up the conversation again and I watched her nodding in response to their statements. I sat wondering if she was ever going to be ready to go when the waitress touched me on the arm.

"Your mother, she is?" I nodded. "She is wonderful. Delightful."

I nodded. "Yeah. She has her moments."

Maybe this kind of interaction was her way to make up for lost time--the last time she was here, she didn't hang out in restaurants chatting up the locals. So I decided to screw Dad's "keep your mother safe" directive. I made that my daily mantra, hoping that by the time I returned home, I would work up the fortitude to shrug off any attempted guilt trip. It could happen.

Heidelberg, Germany

"It's going to be fourteen days. That's the longest I've ever gone without sex." Mom says to me.

We're walking down a cobblestone street outside of Heidelberg, Germany, a picturesque town that has exchanged its prestige for tourists. We're planning to tour the town's pride and joy; a centuries-old castle that stands guard over the small village. It's beautiful, ancient and $20 for the guided tour. Since the tiny bus doesn't depart up the winding drive for an hour or so, we decide to make good use of the time by wandering the streets of the quaint village. History is everywhere--some of it real, some a fictional facsimile of what the Germans think the town looked like in the years before capitalism and that pesky inconvenience called World War Two.

"That's nice, Ma," I tell her, mainly because there's no other way to respond to your mother chatting you up about her sex life.

"Because, really, this is the first long trip I ever took without your father," she says. She stops every couple of steps to gaze into the shop windows that line the cobblestone avenues, so it's taken us about ten minutes to go half a block. "And sex in a hotel is more fun than sex at home."

"Mmmm." I wasn't touching this conversation with ten-foot pole.

"Oh! That's pretty!" she meandered over to the window of yet another shop and stood scrutinizing the cuckoo clocks.

"Maybe I shouldn't have bought that other clock," she sighed. "Look at this one! Isn't it pretty? I like it better than the one I bought."

"Ma, it's just buyer's remorse. You bought yourself a class-A cuckoo clock." I looked at my watch again and felt slightly dismayed that only ten minutes had passed since the last time I checked. Funny how time warps itself in exactly the opposite direction than what you hope for. Like when you are on a bad date and you find yourself sitting across from some loser wishing to God that the hands on the clock above the bar will speed up like they do in a cartoon so when you say, "Wow. I didn't know it was so late! I've gotta run," you won't be lying.

The cuckoo clock she's talking about is the one that we just spent over an hour purchasing. The great cuckoo clock adventure began when we left the hotel with a mission: buy a clock. Not just any clock. A hand-carved cuckoo clock made in the Black Forest. Her insistence bordered on an obsession. Moments after stepping outside of the hotel, we passed our first clock shop.

"Here's a good one, Ma," I said, trying to be helpful.

"No."

"What? Why? Look, Ma, tons of clocks."

"No it's not that, but look at the salesman."

"Yeah?"

"He's Asian. Asians don't make German clocks. We need to find a German."

"A German cuckoo clock maker who lives in the Black Forest?"

She nodded. How hard could this be? We're in Germany. The Black Forest is around here somewhere. I haven't been there yet, but behind the hotel is a cluster of trees and a forest is, by definition, a cluster of trees. It's not like there's going to be any yellow plastic tape strung across two street lamps announcing DO NOT CROSS--BLACK FOREST.

"Why the Black Forest?" I asked out of curiosity as we inch our way along the sidewalk. Mom can't walk as quickly as I can, so I wait for her to complete a full step before I take half of one.

"Because when your Uncle Jerry was stationed in Germany, he bought your grandmother a cuckoo clock made in the Black Forest and I've always wanted that clock. It was beautiful."

"I'm sure there's other clocks that are just as nice. Look here." We'd gone about ten yards and already we stood in front of another clock store.

She stared in the window for a few minutes, pondering the possibilities. "Those are nice," she nodded. "Let's go in."

I held the door for her to enter. She took one step and nodded politely to the man behind the counter. She leaned into me and whispered, "He looks German."

Blonde hair, stout build and bad teeth. "Yep, sure does," I whispered back.

She strode to the counter. "I'd like to look at your cuckoo clocks."

The man smiled broadly, nodded and said something in an accent so thick you could cut it with a spork.

"He sounds, German, too," she whispered.

The blonde man with the German accent gently laid a clock on the counter. Mom examined it for a moment and pronounced her judgment. "Beautiful."

He started extolling the pros of the clock; how it's made from genuine porcelain this, honest-to-god German that. I tried to tune him out. To me, a clock's a clock. If you need one that badly, go to Goodwill and scour the Housewares department. There's a lot of junk people get rid of at Goodwill. Besides, I'm from Seattle, where only Los Angeles transplants buy NEW stuff. Seattleites are more concerned with saving the environment by reusing non-recyclables. I roll this idea over in my mind and wonder if a cuckoo clock made by a genuine German living in the Black Forest is something that a person would bequeath to the Goodwill. Apparently, a Black Forest-made clock touched by real German hands is a commodity. Maybe I should have been a clock maker. I mean, when I was young I looked German. Who would know?

Mom look pleased as she fingered the clock's intricate carvings like they were made from crystal. She nodded. She smiled. Mom smiling is a good thing. The woman shops so much that very little impresses her anymore. When it comes to sniffing out a bargain, she was born with the nose of a bloodhound and the soul of Ebenezer Scrooge.

The man explained the details of the clock while Mom nodded: The chains were silver-plated alloy, as were the heavy counter-weights in the shape of pine cones. The design of the house part of the clock was modeled after traditional German cottages. The roof was an overlay of balsa wood, while the wood of the cottage is maple.

"So it's not made locally?" Mom asks. I can tell by the way her eyes caress it and she uses her pinky to touch the tiny bird that pops out of the small door that she likes it.

"It's assembled in Berlin," he said to her.

"It's a beautiful clock," she said to him, "but I think I'd like to finish shopping first. Thank you for your time." That's the cool thing about Mom--she puts a salesman through the hoops, but she's always polite about rejection.

"Anyone can buy a clock built in a factory," she explains to me as we leave the store. "I want something locally made. I didn't come to Europe so I can buy stuff that I could have ordered over the internet."

We shuffle onward down the uneven sidewalk. I can't argue with her logic. I remember feeling betrayed our first day of the trip--last week--when we arrived in London. We had descended on the rented apartment several hours earlier than expected, sparking chaos. The four Japanese tourists who thought they had secured the apartment through that evening stared at us four Americans standing on the porch, bags in hand. There was much chattering in Japanese and so much bowing I felt light headed. I pointed to the four of us, mimed sleeping and gestured to the apartment. Somehow they were able to decode my theatrics and understood what we wanted. They nodded and bowed some more before disappearing inside, taking our bags with them.

"Well," I said turning to the group. "I'm guessing they're either pilfering through our belongings, or telling us that we've got the place."

"Let's go bumming around London! We can find a mall and do some shopping." Mom's voice always lifted an octave when the word "shopping" was uttered.

"Ma," I sighed, "this is the land of Shakespeare, the Queen and Big Ben. I'm not going to a mall."

"Oh, give me a break, you snob. It's just a couple of hours."

Within the hour we found ourselves wandering an enclosed, generic structure that looked exactly like Every Mall, U.S.A. While the other three were off doing God knows what, I spied a tea shop. Perfect! My friend Crystal was a tea drinker and I was in desperate need of a British souvenir for her.

"I'm visiting," I said to the saleswoman who looked too young to work legally, "from the U.S."

"I can tell from your accent. Chicago?"

I marveled at her. Most Americans can't find England on a map and she could identify me just from a few words. "Yeah. I'm wanting to ship some tea to my friend. Do you have a gift box with a huge variety of British tea, but small enough that it's not going to cost a fortune to mail?"

"Well," she said, popping some gum--seems New York doesn't have the patent on sales people popping gum, "why don't you just order it over the internet?"

"Yeah, I could, But I was hoping to send her something from London. You know, as opposed to some trinket cranked out in China."

"It'll be cheaper."

I thought about her suggestion to save some money and for a moment, the miserly facet of my personality was tempted to throw authenticity to the wind and charge down the Road Cheaply Traveled. But then I felt myself succumb to that human urge that requires us to take a piece of where we've been. That voice that says, "Ah-ha! Welcome to the moon! Now--stick a flag in it!" or "You must strap a video camera to your head for the next 47 hours of your vacation and tape every church, waterfall, birdbath, bathtub and street sign you pass!" Seriously--it's not enough to leap around the lunar surface with an NBC camera trained on you? Apparently not. And how many people return home, pop a bowl full of popcorn, sink into the couch and say, "Rewind to the little kid picking his nose outside the Globe Theatre. Ah! There's a memory.

"Ah, that's okay," I said to the sales girl, vowing to have a piece of Great Britain sent to America, "I really want a souvenir from the UK." How much could it cost to ship? It's only tea.

"Okay." She rolled her eyes and guided me to a display. She babbled on about the tea, sounding very knowledgeable, but I didn't really understand her. I'm a coffee drinker. All I know about tea is that it's a leaf that you dunk in water and load down with sugar, honey and milk to make it taste like something you want in your mouth. Besides, I love the lilt and rhythm of British English. The Brits need to record their best and brightest stage actors talking about something boring--like tea--and sell it to Americans with insomnia. Those CD's will outsell Ambien.

"How long will this take to get there?" I asked, giving her my charge card. By the time she rang up the purchase, added tax and shipping, I paid more for these chopped up leaves than I expected and was smarting a bit. How heavy can a bunch of leaves be, anyway? Apparently a hell of a lot more than ground-up beans.

"Well, you should know, you're American. It'll be shipped out of our supply warehouse in Ohio. How long will it take to go from Ohio to Kentucky?"

I stood dumbfounded. I just paid half a day's salary for something to be mailed from Cleveland? "British tea from the United States?"

"Our teas come in through the central distribution system in Quebec."

"British tea from the United States, via Canada. Wow. I was hoping for something . . . you know . . . authentically British."

She laughed. "Told you it would be cheaper over the internet."

So I could hardly blame Mom for wanting to buy an authentic, German-made cuckoo clock. Who wants a Black Forest cuckoo clock shipped from Cleveland?

"Let's try here," Mom said. I looked up to see her pointing to yet another cuckoo clock store. While my mind has a tendency to boomerang into the past, Mom's mind stays rooted in the present. Maybe this is why I talk about memories while Mom talks about the world using present tense.

As soon as we entered the shop, I knew this place was different from the other cuckoo clock pushers. It didn't reek of Lysol and sterility like some of the tourist traps who cater to Americans. Nor did it try to mask its air with a tacky air freshener that's trying to convince you that you're in a pine forest. This one had a thick, woodsy smell that landed somewhere between "Lumberjack" and "Wet Lumber". Pieces of half-carved wood lay about the work counter amongst carving tools, tiny mounds of sawdust beneath them. We had stepped into a Twilight Zone episode--walked through the door of a tiny Heidelberg boutique and entered a tiny cuckoo clock slaughter house. Indirect sunlight bounced off the surrounding buildings, giving it a tranquil, peaceful ambiance.

"Can I help you?" The dark-haired man behind the counter asked. His English sounded clipped and precise, like the careful pronunciation of a non-English speaker. He might be authentically German. This was a good sign. I crossed my fingers.

Mom explained what she was looking for and he lead her through the maze of display shelves to a section of the shop where a tiny wall stood hidden behind clock parts. The rows of the little black houses ticked erratically, the little arms swinging in syncopation while their brass chains tinkled. As the salesman explained the specifics of the clocks, Mom examined them carefully.

I envied her dedication to shopping. To her, choosing where to put your money is a religious experience; an act that must be contemplated with focus of mind that borders on the holy. Mom is a shopkeeper's nightmare. Her mastery at examining every aspect of a potential purchase is worthy of its own reality TV program. My idea of shopping is running into a store, grabbing the first thing that catches my eye and dashing out. I often timed myself; any transaction lasting over ten minutes was a failure, a sure sign of my incompetence to resist the capitalistic attempts to part me and my money. While watching her approach buying souvenirs on this trip, it has become clear to me that one must know what one wants from their shopping experience in order to make choices one doesn't regret. Knowing that you want to spend your money and time on a cuckoo clock made in the Black Forest by an authentic German gives Mom a goal, a vision, a mission by which she can gauge her success and, therefore, feel satisfied. Knowing what you want makes all the difference in the world.

It dawned on me that shopping is a metaphor for my life. I have always snatched up the first thing I saw laying around without the slightest thought as to what I was grabbing. "If it looks good, go for it"--that was my motto. Sure, one can stumble onto a great bargain along the way, but what was I not seeing as I grabbed the nearest shiny object? Maybe I've been spending my life missing great opportunities not due to some divine plan, but because I'm always taking the Road Easiest Traveled. I've become this post-modern Couch Potato, flipping through the channels of LIFE TV watching what everyone else is doing because I don't have the ability to stop. Look. Think. Choose.

Who knew a cuckoo clock could spawn such deep introspection?

Mom wound up buying two cuckoos that day; one for herself and one for my sister. She still has the clock. So does my sister.

***

"Can you imagine living here?" Mom asked me as we passed the castle. "Getting up to pee at night must have been a bitch."

"If you don't know about indoor plumbing, how can you miss it?" I reminded her.

"Still," she said, her head moving back and forth like a bobble-head, "they had to have hated getting up at night. Freeze your too-too off."

The castle that stands overlooking Heidelberg dates back to the 13th Century. Since that time, it has withstood fires, wars, partial reconstruction and American tourists. The citadel has seen thousands of visitors and been the star of films, photos and documentaries. My mother notices the bathrooms. I'd poke fun at her, but the embarrassing truth is, I was thinking the same thing. The toilet I saw was a small room the size of a guest closet. In the chamber was a raised stone platform. On the stone platform was a smooth piece of wood with three holes cut out. Apparently, after doing their business, the user would then pour water down the hole, adding a twist to that song, "Wash that man right out of my hair"--only this wasn't run-of-the-mill-Rapunzel hair. I didn't think twice about the contraption, to tell you the truth. I'm not that interested in bathroom history.

"That castle is a true German. This is why we come to Europe. See truly German stuff."

Who knew that authenticity was so important to my mother? There was no way in hell she would meander throughout Europe buying products that could just as easily been found in Chicago. The same held true for the restaurants. The more unpronounceable the cuisine, the higher the ranking on the "We Must Eat Here" list. According to Mom, the food we ate had to be unique to the locale in which we ate, so, naturally, my penchant for eating "traditionally American" salads, grilled fish and veggies was a great annoyance to her.

"For God's sake, you can get a salad back home!"

"I like salads," I would respond. This was our dialogue: critique, defense, comment. When one's away from home, it's comforting to know some family dysfunctions can still be obeyed.

"Besides, Ma, I don't want to go home after a trip to Europe and go on a diet."

"Diet, schmiet," she would say, "you're only in Europe once! Eat the damn food!"

I nodded mutely, as--let's face it--when's the last time anyone really won an argument with his mother? I ate the salads anyway, admiring everyone else's ability to chow down on creamy sauces, fat sausages and thick gravy while not giving a crap about how much weight they gained. I have always been one of those people who eats a gluten-free, made-with-Nutrasweet cookie and watches as it super-glues itself to my gut. The polite term is "spare tire", but those of us with the metabolisms of a snail must face the music sooner or later; we don't have a spare tire as much as we carry the whole freaking bus. Some people dream of doing great things. I dream of fitting into the same pair of jeans for more than one summer.

The Battle-To-Put-The-Kibosh-On-Jenny Craig would come to an abrupt end one week later when I surrendered any delusion that I would someday sport six-pack abs. A huge steel kegger? Definitely. Three or four days after Mom caught the Lufthansa flight back to the states, I was snoozing away on the bench of a speeding train as the surprisingly comfortable sleeper car rocked through the southern part of Switzerland. I awoke starving (as usual) so I waddled off in search of something to eat. The dining car lay nearly empty. The sole employee caught my attention first--a heavy-set Italian man with thick, black hair and a five o'clock shadow accentuating his jawline. His white shirt may have been pristine that morning, but by this time of the afternoon, it had one foot in haberdashery heaven; the tails were pulled out of his trousers and stains spotted the front from neck to waist. His olive skin was the perfect backdrop for his teeth, making them seem less yellow than they were.

Standing in front of him at the counter was a handsome couple; the woman thin with a long blonde mane and a man who combed his hair over the bald spot at the crown of his head. They clung to each other with a pornographic urgency and kissed between sentences. They reeked of alcohol. I would like to imagine them as a newlywed couple lost in romantic passion of their honeymoon. The truth was probably that they were bored American suburbanites playing hooky from their Lexus SUV by drinking their way through Europe with all the maturity of snookered college co-eds.

"Don't you have a green salad?" I could barely hear the woman's breathy voice over the knocking of the train against the track.

Mr. Italy nodded furiously. "Of course! The most freshest of the vegetables we have!" I was impressed by his enthusiastic attempt at American.

"A salad, I think," she asked, rubbing her hand along the man's ass. "Not too much dressing. Can I get it on the side?"

"A side?" Mr. Italy's smile faltered.

"Yes, please." Ms. Blonde didn't catch Mr. Italy's furrowed brow. That's the curious thing about Americans. They bitch about tourists from other countries not attempting to speak English, but don't bother bringing a foreign language dictionary with them on their jaunts. The double standard could be seen as naive if it wasn't for the fact that in this 21st Century, any foreign language dictionary is an iPhone application away.

"Not on the salad," I explained, trying to be helpful while Ms. Blonde and Mr. Ass exchanged some spit. "She wants it separate."

"Separate from the salad?" He looked horrified. I nodded. "Oil and the vinegar made here by the chef. It go onto the lettuce of the salad."

"NO!" Ms. Blonde, shrieked as if someone suggested she exchange her Nordstrom purse for a shopping bag. "The calories!"

"Just on the side," Mr. Ass snapped like he was training a dog.

Mr. Italy looked to me and I shrugged.

"I want a hot dog, hold the bun," Mr. Ass quipped before diving into Ms. Blonde's mouth again.

"We have bread," Mr. Italy said, pulling at a bag.

"No," Mr. Ass explained in the same condescending tone. "Hold the bun."

"He means no bread. Just the sausage," I quipped. I was hungry and didn't give a shit whether they thought me rude or not. They may be too busy to rise above trailer park behavior, but I had just waked up from a comfortable nap and have had neither coffee nor food. I was a dangerous weapon.

Mr. Italy placed the anemic hot dog and a bowl of lettuce on the counter, took their money and the lip-swapping duo staggered off to suck more face. Mr. Italy turned to me, sighed and shook his head.

"The food needs the spice," he said to me. "Food is for life. You must have spice in life. Americans have no spice. How can they have a life?"

I instantly thought of my mother and her admonishments of my food choices. I, too, have been traveling throughout Europe, visiting countries I have only read about, just like Mr. Ass and Ms. Blonde. I, too, have been paying more attention to the scale than my sense of adventure. My body may be in Italy, but my mind was firmly planted on Jenny Craig's promise of looking like Valerie Bertinelli, post Eddie Van Halen.

"I'll take a salad, too, please," I said with a shrug. "But I want the dressing all over the lettuce."

Turns out the dressing was a tasty concoction that smacked like a marriage of Italian, Balsamic Vinaigrette and spicy tomato. I have no idea what it was called, but I remember how delicious it tasted on the crisp vegetables. Jenny may have disapproved, but screw her and Valerie--it was worth it.

I hate when Mom is right.

***

"I still can't get over those bathrooms," Mom said as we boarded the shuttle back to the town. "It reminds me of camping."

"What's with you and bathrooms?" I sat watching the tour guide pointing to various attractions along the road as the bus bounced along the uneven road. In one tour alone, I heard that woman speak in German, French and broken English, moving between them with more ease than most of my students use their native tongue. I marvel at how lucky the Europeans are; they live in an area where the countries are so closely knit together that they can pick up another's dialect as easily as we would change the channel on the remote. My last attempt at a spoken language was in high school with a teacher I affectionately referred to as Frau Cow. An obese woman, she carried herself with all the grace of the love child of a Sumo Wrestler and Nurse Ratched.

"Well, haven't you noticed over here how it costs to get into the bathrooms?" she asked. How could I not? I live in Seattle. We drink more coffee than water. We drink so much coffee, we fund the entire South American coffee export industry. I would sooner go broke on this trip paying to use the toilet than buying souvenirs.

"I don't mind paying for toilets here. The restrooms are REALLY clean." She nodded her head to emphasize how clean they were. "You could eat off the floors."

"That's a bad visual picture, Ma." Some mental pictures should stay undeveloped on the darkroom floor.

"I mean, after anyone goes and does their business, some person goes in there and tidies it up. Don't they do that in the men's room?"

I don't remember those kind of things. With all due respect to Senator Larry Craig, I don't usually hang out in public bathrooms. Taking a photojournalistic tour of the men's room never figures into my travel plans.

"Well, in the women's they do," she said. "I don't mind paying to go if someone's going to keep it clean. It keeps someone in a job. You have to admit taking money for the restroom is better than being out of work, or living on welfare. I have to hand it to them--I don't want to clean my own bathroom. Why should I want to clean someone else's?"

She had a point. I have a friend who gets her house cleaned monthly, mainly because she doesn't want to clean her shower. I've asked her why she just didn't do it herself and save the money. A shower is a shower. It's not like a truck wash or a maternity ward where you have to deal with oil, grease or afterbirth.

"It's just gross," she told me.

"So's wiping your ass, but you have to do that, too."

She threw something at me--keys I think. "You're just sick."

"When I was growing up, we had pay toilets," Mom said. "I always thought it was a rip-off. But here, you get something for your money."

"Isn't the privilege to pee enough of a reward?"

"Funny," she chastised. "Next time, look at the bathroom. It's so clean."

***

Having learned my lesson about food somewhere in Switzerland aboard the Germany-Italy train, when I arrived in Cinque Terre, a rugged region of northern Italy, I did what Mom had suggested and paid attention to the bathrooms. The toilet in the hostel was nothing to write home about--the usual small room with a sink and a commode; white, sterile and boring. The water worked and the toilet flushed.

On my second night, after a two-mile hike across a goat path from one of the small villages to the next, a plate of spaghetti and meatballs accompanied by a couple bottles of wine was just the ticket I needed to feel human again. About half an hour later, my bladder was so full I barely made it to the "bathroom"; a 4X4 wooden shed on a slight rise a few yards from the restaurant. The room had no door, just a narrow entryway that faced away from the restaurant and towards the sparkling blue waters of the Mediterranean. The floor of the shed was made of concrete and sloped like a funnel from the four corners, convening at a hole in the floor. Suddenly the boring toilet in the hostel looked much more interesting. As I urinated, I felt very lucky I was a man. I thought about Mom's fascination with bathroom facilities and understood why a clean bathroom must mean so much to a woman over fifty.

Too bad the iPhone hadn't been invented yet. I would have taken a picture for her.

***

Throughout the first week of our trip, I had gotten into the habit of paying with everything with a credit card. I don't normally like to live on plastic because, frankly, the easiest way to destroy a wonderful vacation is to arrive home and look at the Visa bill that arrives in the mail the next month. To me, it's the financial equivalent to waking up with Coyote Ugly; every romantic memory has just been replaced by cursing and banging your head against the wall condemning yourself for not being more fiscally responsible. That being said, I have to admit that the easiest way to see Europe is on the back of a Visa card. Instead of feeling stupid when you don't know what the hell a "quid" looks like, you simply reach into the wallet, dig out the plastic and SHAZAM! Like magic, all your problems are solved.

Until I tried to Visa my way through Heidelberg, Germany.

We had returned from our quest to find the perfect cuckoo clock filled with the thrill of accomplishment. Mom got her dream cuckoo while secure in the knowledge that she haggled a damn good deal from an authentic German cuckoo clock maker. All was right in the world. So while the rest of the group waited for the city bus which would take us to dinner, I excused myself so I could dash across the street to the German equivalent of a Walgreen's and get a snack. I ran into the sterile white market, grabbed my purchase and headed to the cash register. I glanced out the window to make sure the bus hadn't arrived--unlike any other country in the world, German busses are punctual. I was in luck, as the three of them were still standing at the bus stop; although Mom didn't stand as much as she paced.

The sales clerk said something to me in German.

"Excuse me?" I asked, cursing myself for leaving my cheat sheet of German phrases with Mom.

The young clerk scowled at me and repeated herself while waving my charge card in my face. Her jaw was set and her eyes squinted--never a good sign. She shook her head slowly, like she had just sucked on a lemon. I shrugged.

"What?"

She rolled her eyes and started spewing German to me again. Damn! Why didn't I listen to Frau Cow more intently?

"I am sorry," I spoke slowly and clearly, "I don't understand. Sprechen sie English?" I knew I was pronouncing this one correctly. "Do you speak English?" is the only phrase I took away from Frau Cow. Everything else sounded like I was hacking up a lung. That's the problem with German--it may make sense linguistically, but unless you have a hair ball stuck in the back of your throat, it's almost impossible to get the dialect right.

She shouted and waved to someone standing behind what I assumed was the customer service counter. A bulky man with a stern look waddled towards us, sporting the same lemon-sucking face as the clerk. I glanced outside again. I didn't want the others to miss the bus on my account. I wish I could say it was because of my kind, altruistic nature not wanting to disrupt my mother's adventure. The truth is that if we missed the bus because of a bag of nuts, I'd never hear the end of it. Luckily, the three figures were still waiting at the bus stop; two sitting calmly and the third spinning around, looking at the buildings, gesturing to the sky . . . like I said--there's comfort in familiarity.

The man said something. I didn't understand the words, but the tone was unmistakable: What kind of idiot are you? I looked at him.

"I'm sorry. I don't understand." I gestured to my temple and shook my head. Either he was going to deduce I didn't speak German, or that I had just lost my mind. Either interpretation was correct.

The man and the young girl looked at each other and shook their heads. Then, they started talking in German again--really fast and with a curt, abrupt tone that told me they were pissed off. About what for God's sake? I happened to glance down and saw they were looking at the back of my Visa, where I had written the words: PLS SEE I.D. where the signature is supposed to go.

"Oh!" I finally got the problem. "Yes. That is me." I whipped out my passport and showed it to them. They recoiled from it. Apparently I look like the kind of guy who would steal an American Visa card to buy some nuts. The young woman yanked the Visa away from me like the passport would taint its value. She said something to the man. He nodded and walked away. Then he picked up the phone. Crap! He was calling the police. Well, maybe the police spoke English. Then again, maybe the police would arrest me and throw me in the German penitentiary for the rest of my life. I wondered it German prisons resembled the ones in Turkey, like in that movie *Midnight Express*. I hope not. I hate naked yoga and getting raped in the shower.

I looked at Mom again. She was standing at the bus stop, waving to me. The bus must be on its way. I waved back to her through the glass doors and mouthed: Help. She shrugged: What's going on? I motioned for her to come into the store: Get in here, I'm about to be arrested and thrown into a German prison for trying to steal some cashews. She waved back: The bus is coming, get over here. I motioned harder and with larger arm movements: Get in here and save me from the lemon-sucking duo who want to throw me into a German prison! She threw up her hands in disgust and pointed towards what must have been the bus rapidly approaching. I walked to the door, intent on shouting at her when I heard the gruff voice of the man behind the counter. He didn't sound happy. I turned to him and saw him motioning for me to move away from the door. Great. Now they can get me for fraud and evading the police.

"My mom," I said to the girl, "that's my mom. Mutter." I pointed to Mom, who was still gesturing to the invisible bus and motioning me to get a move on.

"Never mind," I said, pushing the purchase back towards the girl. "I'll pay cash." I took out my wallet. No money. It was then I remembered I had spent the last of my cash at the castle with the fascinating toilet. Damn--I knew paying with cash would come back to haunt me. I turned back to the window. Outside, the bus was standing at the stop and people were getting off. My three companions stood staring at me through the store window.

"Forget it," I said, pointing to the purchase. "No. Me. No. Want." What is it about attempting a foreign language that turns us all into a character from *Clan of the Cave Bear*?

The man hung up the phone and returned to the dour-looking sales girl. They said something and looked at my credit card again. Just then the door to the shop opened and Mom entered.

"What the hell are you doing?" She demanded.

I instantly turned into a blithering idiot. "They aren't taking my card, they think I stole it, I don't know what's going on."

"Pay cash."

"I don't have any."

"Oh, for Christ's sake," She said, opening her purse. She counted out some marks and shoved them across the counter to the girl, who stood there glaring at me.

As the girl stood evaluating Mom's potential as a dangerous cashew-stealing American, Mom snatched the card away from her and gave it back to me. The man started to say something, and Mom shook her head at him. She pointed to me, then held one finger to her head and motioned: Crazy.

"My son," She said, shaking her head at me. "Dumpkauf." The man laughed. The young woman handed Mom back her change and smiled.

"Danke."

"Danke," Mom replied. Then to me, "Come on. We already missed one bus waiting for you. Jesus Christ, what the hell are you doing without any cash on you?"

I slinked behind her, clutching my purchase like a toddler would a toy bear. As I left, I noticed the man and salesgirl laughing and pointing at me.

"I told you--always keep some cash on you."

"I know."

A day or two later, Mom sat on her bed in the hotel, struggling with the phone. I helped her connect to the international operator and left her alone. When I returned to check up on her, I entered just as she said, ". . . and your idiot son is running around without any cash on him."

"Mom, are you talking to Dad?"

"Yes. And he wants to talk to you."

Amsterdam

"Mom, do not tell Dad that you went into a hash bar," I said.

"Oh, pooh," Mom said.

"You're going to narc on me, aren't you?"

"You worry too much."

"He'll accuse me of not watching out for you. He'll blame me for turning you into a hash whore or something."

"Oh, he won't blame you," she assured me. "You worry too much about what your father is going to say."

She was right, of course, and I knew it. She had breeched this subject several years previously, on our first vacation together in New York for my birthday. I skirted the issue of my hyper-sensitive relationship with Dad back then, but maybe now was the time to tell her why when Dad points his finger at me and says, "She's your responsibility", I suddenly feel like I'm ten. I should probably explain to her why when she narced on me to him about drying her body with Belgian paper towels, I began to hyperventilate. But looking up at the blue spring sky, hearing the sounds of laughter and birds and smelling the tangy scent of hash made me change my mind. This kind of parent/child chat could wait. In all honesty, I couldn't really expect her to keep these things from Dad, as much as I wanted her to do so. She naturally wanted to share her excitement with her husband. It's not her fault her husband had the adventurous spirit of a houseplant.

So instead of opening the door to a deep, compassionate, adult-oriented discussion with my mother, I contemplated the pros and cons of having Mom visit a hash bar. On the PRO side: People would be so much nicer to deal with than they are when they don't visit a hash bar; in Amsterdam, it isn't a long walk to find a hash bar, therefore, not likely to stumble into a bad neighborhood and die in a drive-by shooting; you can sip a nice cup of coffee while sucking down a doobie--considered (in some circles) to be Nirvana. On the CON side: Dad would be disappointed in me. Once again, I would defy his request to give Mom the kind of vacation he thinks she should have in favor of the one I think she should have. Maybe he'll buy into the hash bar visit if I tell him that they're just as popular as Niagara Falls and The Tower of London. Somehow in Dad's book, I suspected "hash bar" fell slightly below "taking your mother to a gay bar" and slightly above "being sold a vibrator by a gay guy in leather chaps and jockstrap".

Ironically, the day had started out so mundanely. Mom and I had wandered off down the winding streets of Amsterdam without an agenda, determined to roam the city with the type of crazed abandon envied by both naive high schoolers and senile senior citizens. We had meandered through alleys, across cobble-stoned courtyards speckled with tiny cafe tables, and streets packed with bicycles. The canal twinkled with reflected sunlight and a cool breeze tickled our hair. The sun was shining, the people we met smiled at us and a great percentage of them held the doors open as Mom barreled into shops.

As we passed a series of stone buildings on our quest for yet another authentic Amsterdamian souvenir, I caught a whiff of a familiar scent--one I hadn't smelled since . . . oh . . . last month. I was a Theatre major, after all, thereby giving me inalienable rights to personal experiences and a vast array of random facts about illegal drugs. Sometimes cliches are true.

"What's that?" Mom asked, sniffing the air like a bloodhound on the trail of prey.

I gestured to the innocuous looking building to our right while I leaned over and whispered to her, "It's probably the hashish bar."

Mom froze. She cocked her head to one side and squinted at me. "A wha-?"

"Hash bar." I said. "Hash is . . ." I couldn't figure out what to tell her. As far as I know, her only exposure to drugs was the Nyquil in her bathroom. "It's like marijuana."

I knew it was the wrong thing to say as soon as the smile spread across her face. "Let's go!" She giggled in glee.

"No."

"But, David, I have never seen a hashis bar."

"Neither have I," I said, pulling her along. "And it's hash-SHEESH. Not hashis."

"We'll just tell them I need to use the bathroom then," she said, heading for the door. "They won't tell an old lady she can't use the bathroom."

"You're going to lie about having to pee just so you can sniff hash?"

"No, I really do need to go. I'm old. Old people need to go all the time. Don't you watch those commercials on incontinence?"

"Mom," I started to protest, but she already had my elbow in a vice-like grip and was steering me to the door. "They're probably stoned anyway, so they'll never know if I used the bathroom or not."

I was ready to put my foot down and, if necessary, go toe-to-toe with her like a couple of white trash hooligans fighting over a sweater sale in the local Walmart, but I was too stunned by the facts that she knew the term "stoned" and used it correctly in a sentence. What's the story with parents these days? Where do they learn this stuff? In seconds she was across the crowded sidewalk and pushing through the door, tickling the little bell over the entryway which announced that another toker was in the building.

Being an American on my first trip to Amsterdam, I had never been in a real live hash bar before, college dorm rooms not withstanding. In my mind, a hash bar was half speakeasy and half holding cell at the city jail; a sleazy, dimly-lit, dirty room with people sitting alone in the dark, cigar-sized joints in hand, wheezing into scarves while sitar music played quietly in the background. Reefer Madness on steroids. True to my life story, reality is much more mundane than my imagination. The hash bar more closely resembled the coffee shops in Seattle than a scene from *Scarface*. It was a well-lit, rectangular room with cafe tables lining one wall and a long glass display case filled with pastries opposite. Several people of various ages occupied tables decked out with chess games, Scrabble and various newspapers. Amsterdam hash bars are European Starbucks, only their tobacco is less expensive than a venti, non-fat soy latte. Noticeably absent was the infamous smokable weed. Where did they store the hash? At Starbucks, I can see the coffee.

We sidled up to the counter where a huge blackboard spanned the entire back of the bar. I saw the words, but had no idea what they hell they meant. Sure, I knew *Columbian* and *Acapulco Gold*, but what the hell were these other kinds? I scanned the list and nodded convincingly. If there's one thing I can do extraordinarily well, it's faking competence. I leaned over to Mom, nodding to the numerous words written on the blackboard and whispered, "See those names?"

"Yeah," she whispered back through the side of her mouth. To those who knew us, we looked like ordinary mother and son. To those who didn't, we looked like two Secret Service members minus the dark shades, earpieces and president. All the subtleties of a freight train, my mom and I.

"Those are the names of the different kinds of dope."

"Where's the dope?" Mom asked.

"That's what I'm wondering."

Mom smiled at the dope barista, a handsome young man with thick black hair and a smile that got him anything he wanted.

"BATHROOM?" Mom yelled. This is another trick Mom learned while in Europe. If you don't speak the language, yell louder.

Mr. Million Dollar Smile nodded and pointed to the back of the room. "THANK YOU," Mom shouted, and wiggled her fingers in a small wave as she hobbled to the back of the place, stumbling along slowly enough to inhale twice as often as necessary on the way. Great. Now she'll be stoned. Next thing I know, she'll get the munchies and we'll be forced to stop for Doritos, chocolate and popcorn.

I took a seat off to the side, next to two men with thick beards who spoke in harsh tones, and wide arm gestures. It didn't take fluency in the language to know the conversation was an intense one. I watched their fists pound the air and found myself spinning back in time, wondering where that passionate young man I used to be had gone. Once I used to be like these bearded punch-the-air guys; feeling so strongly about an issue my face flushed, caring so deeply about the human race that my pulse raced erratically. Now, I feet deeply about being in bed by midnight. I care deeply about someone stealing my parking spot. Is that what growing up is about? Exchanging passion for contentment? I wished I could understand their language and eavesdrop on what the heated conversation was about. Politics? The economy? The benefits of Acapulco Gold over Columbian? Although judging by their wide, alert eyes, the benefits of the wacky weed had not fully intruded upon their consciousness. I heard the door chime and a young couple strode in and placed their order. Now was my chance to see where the hash lived! Surely Mr. Million Dollar Smile would reveal the hiding place of the weed now! The worker nodded and began pulling coffee grounds for espressos. Espressos? I'm from Seattle and can see beans and steam any day of the week. I was in a hash bar, for crying out loud. I wanted to see the hash! Luck wasn't on my side, as by the time the drinks were made, Mom had returned from her visit to the loo and stood over me at the table.

"Okay," she said, heading for the door. "See anything?" I shook my head. Mom shrugged.

As we stepped out onto the sidewalk, I turned back to look into the shop through the window. "I'm disappointed that I didn't see any hash."

"I smelled it." Mom said.

"Me, too, but I wanted to see it."

"Ah, well, tough toenails, Tony," Mom responded. "You've seen the hash bar."

I nodded. I suppose she's right. Hash is kind of like believing in God. You don't have to see it to know it exists.

"Still," Mom said in a faraway voice, "we should have ordered some. I've never had hash."

***

"So, you know what we've got see see in Amsterdam?" Mom asked.

"Yeah! Anne Frank's house." I answered.

"No. The red light district."

"You have got to be frickin' kidding me."

"Why?" Mom looked honestly confused. "We're in Amsterdam. We should see the red light district."

"No way."

"Why?"

"I am not taking you to see a bunch of hookers, Ma."

"David," she said sternly, "I know about sex. I've had two children."

I covered my ears and began to hum.

"I'm serious."

"Ma, so am I," I said. "I've already got to explain to Dad why you went into a hash bar. He will <u>never</u> understand why I took you to see hookers."

"Don't tell him."

"I won't! You will!" I knew she would, too. Charlie Brown may never have learned his lesson with Lucy and that damned football, but I only had to endure my father's lectures about being an irresponsible son five or six times before I learned mine.

Later, I told this story to some friends of mine. They were as mystified by my attitude as Mom. Even in retrospect, I stand by my decision. Basically, there were two problems with escorting my Mom to the part of town where working girls worked: First, she's my mother. I'm sure there's a whole PhD dissertation on the apprehensions of a son, his mother and whores and how those three categories apply to the "Madonna/Whore" complex, but there you go. The second reason was more pragmatic--if Dad went bonkers over her chatting up the guy in assless chaps and a dog collar, he would have a coronary about the prostitutes. The dilemma was that Mom made a lot of sense: Going to Amsterdam and not seeing the Red Light District would be like going to New York and avoiding the Empire State Building. You may have no real desire to see the place, but if you don't, you'll always wonder what it looked like.

As fate would have it, about the same time we were discussing the pros and cons of prostitute perusing, we passed a small kiosk with advertisements about sightseeing boats that gave "a breathtaking view of Amsterdam via the canal". I figured it was too good to be true; it must be divine intervention. I could get my mom on a boat, ply her with White Zinfandel and maybe she'd become so sauced, that she'd forget the whole idea was to see some hookers. What could be better than whore-watching from the deck of a ship while chugging a Blue Hawaiian? I bought us two tickets.

That night, while the other two members of our fellowship were left to their own devices, Mom and I walked to the dock and boarded the small boat with a plethora of other middle-aged tourists. I expected the hour-long canal float to be a cross between a geriatric bingo parlor and a funeral barge, but much to my surprise, the ride was geared more towards lazy Americans than elderly shufflers. Fashioned after a miniature old-time ferry boat, the interior cabin housed bench seats for about fifty normal-sized butts, with additional seating above on the open deck for those who liked to freeze to death in the cold spring air. The music was contemporary, the sound system well balanced and the decor crisply modern. Mom and I decided to avoid becoming human slushies and sat below, in the heated cabin next to one of the large windows.

The view of the city from our seats was breathtaking. The illumination from the street lamps, bike lights and neon signs of the surrounding businesses bounced off the wet Cobblestone streets, lighting up downtown with a peaceful glow. The gentle curves of the city's roads radiated outward from the center of town, turning the ancient metropolis into a pinwheel of soft illumination, allowing you to see its edges, but not its center. This was my lesson of Amsterdam: She invites you in, but holds back from revealing too much of herself, challenging you to cross her boundaries and experience her wonders on her terms. Or not. Amsterdam dares you to think about what it is you want. Or not.

From our vantage point, we were close enough to see the faces of the people as they stood on the walkway which paralleled the canal and watched them watching us. Many of our spectators stood touching each other and grinning; not in a sexual groping kind of way, but a friendly holding of hands or a gentle hand along the small of the back of their partner. The scene resembled the throngs of New York, which Mom and I had spent hours analyzing a few years before, with the exception that in New York people looked agitated, hurried and pressured. When you look into the faces of New Yorkers, you see a boiling pot of emotions. When you look into the faces of Amsterdam you see a group of happy, contented people who are thrilled to be alive. That's the difference between America and Europe, Mom and I decided on that trip: Americans rush through life searching for the pot of gold that will make their lives worth living. Europeans know life is worth living even without the gold. Europeans are Human Beings. Americans are Human Doings.

The cruise ended much too early for us. It felt as if no sooner did we settle back with our wine than the boat sidled up to the dock and stopped.

By the time we returned to our hotel, the other two had eaten and were now sitting in the girl's hotel room with a glass of wine in their hands, getting a head start on the nightly buzz. They didn't ask about the trip, nor if we enjoyed ourselves. We didn't volunteer information.

That night, the other two and I hiked over to the Red Light District without Mom. I realize that one should see it for the bragging rights of saying, "I went to the red light district", but it can just as easily be seen in a well-made documentary. The streets of the Red Light District aren't walled off, gated, guarded or monitored by attack dogs in order to prevent naive tourists and innocent children from wandering into the den of carnal lust (as so many pious religious fanatics in America want you to believe). Rather than a maze of sordid, seedy alleyways winding through the landscape of the seven deadly sins, the Red Light District is a well kept, clean and inviting set of five city blocks that sport wide streets filled with pedestrians. The buildings look similar to many other buildings on many other city blocks, only instead of large display windows featuring plastic mannequins clothed in overpriced clothes made in third world countries by slave labor, there are large display windows featuring real women clothed in sexually provocative lingerie. I like to think of it as *Victoria's Secret Meets Disneyland*. Minus the silly mouse ears. In America, the Red Light District would never survive. It would be deemed a surefire sign of the coming apocalypse and the streets would be picketed by prominent heads of church, hellbent on denying that any God-fearing, church-going American ever had a lustful thought. Ironically, if this same district were assigned a TV crew, on-screen host, and an hour on prime time, American networks would call it Reality Drama and show it along with a slew of ads about erectile dysfunction. Overnight we'd have a fleet of planes filled with curious tourists flying out of cornfields all over the midwest, bound for this "new and undiscovered" slice of sin. America. Go figure.

To ensure the attention of the pedestrian traffic is on the women and not the historic buildings or hash bars, the large picture windows are outlined with a string of tubing which houses red neon lights. Behind that glass, framed by red lights, are small 10X10 rooms which contain a couple chairs, a small table and a bed. Hanging out in these doll-like rooms are gorgeous women who sit behind the thick panes of glass and knit. Or read. Or smile and wave to the tourists with coy smiles that look suspiciously like Miss America contestants. It's all very *Mayberry RFD*-ish. It's as if you could walk right into the pseudo-living room with a cup of coffee and a box of cookies and chat about who's going to win *American Idol* this season. The only hint of the room's true purpose was when, as if by a psychic signal, the woman would stand up, pull on a cord and thick, red velvet curtains would close, cutting off the public's view. There was no siren, flashing lights or other Hollywood-esque fanfare. Rather anti-climatic, really.

In retrospect, I wonder what all the fuss was about. The women looked happy to have the chance to catch up on their reading or to complete those socks they were knitting; the streets around the zone were safe, well lit and filled with polite people; the area coffee shops seemed to be doing a bang-up job of perpetuating capitalism and everyone seemed content with life.

Those crazy Europeans.

***

"I don't want you to be upset," I said to Mom, examining her face for any sign of disappointment. That's the thing about mothers--regardless of your age, gender or sexual orientation, they have the power to take you from feeling ecstatic to piece- of-crap-traitor in six seconds.

"I'm not upset," she said, totally expressionless.

"It's just that I really want to take a bike ride and Amsterdam is so bike friendly--" Mom didn't let me finish.

"Go. Go. I'll stay here, rest and read a book. I'm easy. I ain't cheap, but I'm easy."

"I feel so guilty, though. I told Dad I would take care of you--"

She rolled her eyes. "Tough toe nails, Tony. Who's taking care of him?"

I thought about this for a minute. "Considering he's home alone and you're in Amsterdam hanging out in hash bars . . ."

She shooed me towards the door while I continued looking for signs of the Mom Lie--that look a mom gets when she tells her children what she thinks the children want to hear. Most of the time, mothers get a way with the great Mom Lie, as they've been programming their offspring since birth and know every button to push. Sometimes it backfires, though, like in the case of an actor friend of mine, a guy who came from a family so dysfunctional, he could not only identify which things his mother said was a lie, but could describe the facial tick which gave her away. I told him once that his upbringing must have been hell. He disagreed.

"Why do you think I'm such a great sign language interpreter? Passive-aggressive people may be dysfunctional, but it's a hell of a breeding ground for forensic detectives and mimes."

I deduced Mom was telling me the truth. Either she really didn't mind me dumping her so I could aimlessly scour the streets of a foreign city looking for a bike rental, or she has a face that would win the World Poker Tour.

"Okay," I said finally, figuring that if she really did have that great a poker face, she would have worked for a Las Vegas casino rather than the phone company for twenty years. "But don't leave the hotel."

"What am I? Twelve?"

"No, but I don't want to be the one to tell Dad that you were raped and murdered in Amsterdam because I let you out of the hotel without an escort."

She sighed and rolled her eyes. She opened her mouth to protest again, but I pulled the Son Card. The Son Card is a close relative of the Mom Lie, in that it is aimed to comfort the other person. But while the Mom Lie is just that, a lie, the Son Card is more of an adolescent visual whine that enables a son to manipulate a mom into doing a whole variety of things from lending money for some ridiculous frivolity, to not telling dad that the dent in the car was done by the son (not that I have any personal experience in this avenue). I knew using the Son Card was iffy at best, as Mom is impervious to both manipulation and blatant displays of sympathy solicitation, but occasionally it works. Once I brought her chocolate from Chicago's Marshall Fields, and as I handed the gift to her, she asked, "Oh, great. What did you do now?"

This night, I've either hit her at a weak moment, she's feeling particularly nostalgic, or she's tired.

"I'm fine," she agreed. "I'll stay here and read and relax." She shrugged. "I'm easy. I ain't cheap, but I'm easy. Go pedal your ass around Amsterdam."

So we left Mom to her own devices in the hotel room, grabbed our water bottles and headed out to find a bicycle rental place. This was about four in the afternoon. We had no map, but we did have a vague sense of the bike shop being about a mile in a north-easterly direction. We were right, too, as the bike shop was less than a mile from the hotel. And it was in a north-easterly direction. And the bike shop rented with a one hour minimum. Too bad it took us over an hour to find it. I was so caught up in the ambiance of Amsterdam that I forgot a key component to maneuvering the city: it's not laid out in a grid. So here I was, wandering around Amsterdam with no ability to speak Dutch, German, French or Spanish, no map, and trying to find my way around blocks in a city that had no blocks.

We returned to the hotel about seven that evening, exhausted from walking two or three miles only to bike several more. We dragged ourselves up the stairs, our leg muscles screaming, shirts damp with sweat, stomachs growling and annoyed at ourselves for leaving without so much as the hotel's phone number, or the word for *map* in Dutch. We stumbled back to the hotel where we found Mom stretched out on the couch in her nightgown. Candles illuminated the room, giving it a soft, peaceful ambiance and filling the air with a hint of lavender and vanilla. She was reading a book with a glass of wine in her hand and a bag of chocolates in her lap.

"Have fun?" she asked, turning down the television.

I related the tale to her with excruciating detail. In truth, I went on a bit too long about riding the wrong way on a once-way street and nearly being plowed down by cars, but I didn't want her to feel bad about being dumped for the evening.

"I went for a walk," she told me when I finished my tale.

"Mom, damn it, I asked you not to!"

"I knew you'd be upset, that's why I waited for you to get out of sight before I left the hotel."

"You snuck out?"

"It's my vacation, too."

"What if--"

"What if nothing." Mom waved me off. "Will you stop worrying and relax? Jesus Christ Almighty."

"Okay. As of now, I'm worry-free. I'm hungry. Where do you want to go for dinner?" I asked. A shower and some food would was long overdue.

"Already taken care of," Mom said. "Here, hold my wine." I did and she trotted over to the corner and retrieved a huge paper sack. She carried it to the small coffee table and began hoisting food out of the bag. Soon we had a spread of cheese, fruit, bread and potato chips.

"I went past this adorable store and decided to pick us up something to eat."

"Apparently," I said, digging in.

"I figured you'd probably be a while and would be too tired to go out." She settled back into the couch. "Then, on the way back, I passed a wine store and picked up this delicious bottle of wine. Then, I found this candy store." She threw a small bag onto the table. "I picked up a piece for all of you. I ate mine already."

"Did you have supper?"

"Oh, yeah!" She gestured to the trash. "I bought myself some stuff from the deli. I took a bubble bath, lit some candles and kicked back with this wine, chocolate and a good book." She shrugged. "Now I feel clean, fresh and relaxed."

"So while we were wandering the city, going the wrong way on one-way streets and getting lost, you were eating bon-bons and drinking wine."

"Glad we all had a good time," she said, popping more chocolate into her mouth. "See? Everything always works out."

"Yeah," I said.

"Go take a shower. You look dirty and sweaty."

As I headed back to my room, she said, "I'm glad I stayed behind; my foot was starting to hurt. Besides, I would have missed the chocolate."

I looked at her closely. I had to admit--I hadn't a clue as to whether this was a Mom Lie or not. I guess age really does pay off in the long run. Old people have had more time to perfect the poker face.

RELATED TANGENT #4

Many years ago, I heard a story about scientists experimenting with frogs. The story goes like this:

A group of scientists studying frog behavior placed a frog in a petrie dish. As long as it was not directly threatened, the frog sat quietly on its little glass lily pad. Then the petrie was placed over a flame. Still, the frog sat, contemplating its little froggy life. Although the heat intensified, the frog remained unmoving in its familiar surroundings. The scientists watched as the frog slowly cooked, until, finally, one of the scientists thumped the dish--one hopes out of an altruistic desire to save the creature and not out of his/her hatred of a broiled frog legs dinner. Only then did the frog leap from the dish. The scientists hypothesized that only when sudden, unexpected forces intrude upon our otherwise peaceful lives do creatures move to save themselves.

I can't verify this story is true, but since hearing it, my life has made a hell of a lot more sense. It helps me understand how people put up with bad jobs; it sheds light on those pathetic marriages where both people are miserable, yet still stay together. It explains why a friend of mine invited me to dinner and in the middle of the Chocolate Decadent Surprise, she blurted out, "I knew it! I JUST KNEW HE WAS SLEEPING AROUND!" and "I KNEW something was going on! Why am I so gullible? Why didn't I break up with him when you told me to?"

What could I say? "I told you so"? Or spew some pithy line like, "Love is blind"?

Anyone who has ever looked back on their past, slapped themselves on the forehead and screamed, "WHY AM I SUCH AN IDIOT!?!?", never fear. You're not an idiot. Regardless of that gnawing can't-get-this-out-of-my-mind suspicion churning from your gut; regardless of the fact that friends descend upon us for a "relationship intervention" (complete with photos of the lying bastard and sworn testimony from the floozies he's been screwing), people generally won't face the truth if the truth is emotionally painful. Most people endure relationship torture with a stoicism that's the envy of US Marines.

So if you're one of those people who's ever looked facts in the face and said, "Ha! I smite thee down, facts! I will believe what I choose to believe, despite all logic to the contrary, for I am comfortable in my petrie dish! Sure, it's a bit more humid than yesterday, but that's just Global Warming!" Don't kick yourself over your naivety. It's human nature--actually frog nature, but who's fact checking here?--to adapt to anything "different". Just like when we fall in love so hard that we ignore the sociopathic, insane things our lovers do. (Remember: Even Hitler had a girlfriend.)

My hobby is watching people. Over the years I have learned that humans want the things we love to stay with us. We fight like angry pitbulls to make sure the things we love never go away. But at some point, we're all going to get our dish thumped; hopefully it's before we sizzle like a frog over a Bunsen burner.

So on August 1st, 2007, when I held my cell phone to my ear and heard my sister mumble the words, "Are you alone?" I felt my own little petrie dish tremble and the heat increase. I somehow knew in my gut that Dad was dead, but I didn't want to believe it. So I didn't.

For a few minutes denial worked great, until she thumped the dish so hard, I felt my gut fly across the room.

"Yes," I said.

"Dad's dead," She told me. Her voice sounded strained; as if she were on an emotional precipice ready to fall into the abyss.

I don't know exactly how long I lingered in my 8X8 cubicle in the call center, but in all likelihood it was only a few minutes. As I sat there the truth of what she had just said fell into me. Dad's dead. My petrie dish had been thumped.

Ice crawled down my spine and I shivered. I tried to suck in air, but my lungs weren't working. I tried to speak but my mouth refused to function. When I felt I could breath again without fear of vomiting, I cleared my throat.

"Ummma, wumma, wow, dingly-dang."

A rush of nonsensical noise shot out of my mouth instead of the words that I had intended to say. The more I tried to speak, the more I sounded broken, like the treasured heirloom of your mother's that you break and super glue back together, thinking nobody will notice. Which I know nothing about, by the way.

Miraculously, my sister understood my gibberish as actual English sentences.

"Heart attack. In the garage." Her monotone voice responded.

"Umm...wazzie waddle ding dang."

"I'll pick you up at the airport. Let me know when the plane arrives."

I hung up and stared at the cubicle's divider. The fabric that covered the surface of the movable walls was composed of tightly woven threads of canvas. A million thin threads converging together to make something larger than themselves; a covering for a cheaply made, weak piece of furniture whose only purpose was to divide a group of people into individual units where they sat alone in front of a computer, close enough to hear the words of the other people on the floor, but cut off from them. Individual yet collective. Like Dad's tools hanging in the garage above his workbench, each individual tool hanging from its own set of metal hooks--laid out so he could see in a glance what he had available to work with. What the hell were we going to do with his tools? I can't even hammer a nail straight.

I calmly went downstairs, lit a cigarette and called my boss. I needed to have the week off for my father's funeral, as he just died, you see. Do I have some leave time accumulated? Suddenly, I was in her office with her and another staff member, watching them move about the room speaking into the phone, whose long cord wound around them like a viper as they paced before me. My boss thrust a piece of paper into my hand and told me I had an airline reservation.

Suddenly I was one hundred-twenty miles north, standing outside of my townhouse speaking to my neighbor. I stood asking her to watch my cat because I had to fly to Tennessee; my dad just died, you see, so I couldn't feed the cat for a week or so and someone needed to feed her or she'd die. Would that be too much trouble? Then I was at the airport. Instantly, I found myself in Nashville and my sister was waiting for me in her huge-ass, gas-guzzling SUV, outside of the baggage claim. Mom was in the front seat, talking about the warm weather, the possibility of rain tomorrow and, oh, by the way, how was your flight?

"Winnie winnie zip zang."

Mom launched into a monologue, lasting all the way from the Nashville airport to my sister's house. Her voice sounded normal to me; she didn't have the speech defect I was suffering. In fact, she seemed in control to the point of normality. Why she wasn't a babbling blob of tears, when I was such a mess? I hadn't been able to go longer than a couple hours without tearing up, and here Mom was making complete sentences and not a wet eye in the house. Dad just died, for crying out loud. You found him laying on the cement floor of the garage. You bent to shake him and saw that his lips were blue. You were the one to follow the directions of 9-1-1 and give him mouth-to-mouth, to no avail. You did all of this and now you sit in the front seat of a car chatting about the weather? What was wrong with her?

What was wrong with me? This flicker of self-doubt fluttered around my mind a few times and then settled nicely into a previously clean corner of my mind and began eating at my brain. Something must be wrong with me, wasn't there? Death is a reality, just another step on the journey of life. Why couldn't I accept it? There must be something amiss with my emotional development when an adult male who has lived on his own for over twenty years is suddenly hobbled by a natural occurrence. Dad always said take care of her, she was my responsibility, but she apparently wasn't the one who needed the help. It was him all along and somehow I missed that. I fell for the smoke screen and mistook his "Watch out for her" at face value and did so, when I should have been watching out for him, too. I watched Mom speaking, hearing the words coming out of her mouth, but unable to respond. My arm wouldn't work. It remained frozen at my side, unable to process the simple commands my brain shot its way. Because it finally hit me that when I, too, die, my friends would be driving to my cremation, babbling away about God-knows-what just like we were now. Is that what I wanted? Is that what my life is amounting to--a group of people babbling about the weather, the possibility of rain and, oh, yeah, how was your flight? This is what it's all about?

I heard silence and realized Mom had just asked me a question.

"Whuzzz bgt fthlmmph," I responded.

"Oh, good," Mom said.

Then we all sat in silence.

PART THREE: Oprah
Spring, 2008

It was an unusually hot spring afternoon the day I realized I should thank Oprah for reconnecting me with my parents. I'm not sure why I was thinking of Oprah on an unusually hot spring afternoon, as I doubt Oprah did much yard work, much less on hot spring afternoons. Nevertheless, there I was--in Mom's yard working on all those projects Mom had asked me to finish during my week's stay. I was more interested in food, as Mom promised me a big lunch in exchange for the manual labor. Food has always played a disproportionately large role in my family. I envy those families with the celebratory Thanksgiving/Birthday/Christmas kind of food role. My family tended more towards the destructive, "Oh, I'm bored and have nothing to do so I'll eat a box of Oreos" kind of role. Since my parents both worked full time while I was growing up, they were too tired for hiking, biking and skiing, and the X-box hadn't been invented yet, so they exchanged family game time for Mars bars and a TV with a remote. This guilt-induced-food may not have won them the Good Housekeeping Seal of Approval as parents, but since Dad's death, I've periodically come to Mom's to do work around the house, which is always good for lunch and a movie.

(One of the coolest things in life is when your parents retire. They get the rest they deserve, the ability to pursue all those hobbies they've been dreaming about and a discount at Denny's. A convenient byproduct for their children is that they have plenty of time to do things for you. Where you used to buy cookies to bring to a potluck, now all you have to do is ask and WHAM! Tasty homemade treats. Try asking for some brownies next time you visit your mom.)

The day in question, I wandered around to the back porch and peeked in through the sliding glass door to spy on Mom and see what she made for lunch. The table was bare. Mom was nowhere in sight.

I found her sitting in the recliner watching Oprah.

"Your father never liked Oprah very much," Mom said. "But I love her. Do you watch Oprah?"

I nodded and sat down. That's the interesting thing about Oprah--whether you want to watch her show or not, the strength of her personality pulls you into her world like a tractor beam on a distressed Enterprise. Most of the world loves her for her generosity, her ability to get to the truth of an issue or any one of many reasons that put her into a popularity contest with Jesus Christ. Me? Our relationship is a bit more complex. My love/hate relationship with Oprah began in 1985 when I was sitting with my sister and my mother on hard, plastic chairs in the Intensive Care Unit waiting room in a suburban Chicago hospital waiting to find out if my father was going to die. We sat several chairs apart from each other, as if the cheap plastic could symbolize the emotional distance we had all put between ourselves. I stared at the TV as a heavy-set black woman with a booming voice and a wicked smile grinned into the camera. I had no idea who she was, but her energy was infectious and her laughter rang with sincerity.

"Who the hell is this woman?" I asked.

"Oprah."

"Okra?"

"Oprah," Mom corrected. "Like Harpo spelled backwards."

"Oh, Jeez," I whined. "What a moronic name."

"She has this show."

No kidding, I thought. The sound on the TV in the waiting room was turned down, so the only thing I heard was a muffled jumble of indistinguishable words. But the visuals explained everything: Some fat black woman had a talk show where they chatted about fashion. Great. Just what we need. Another bimbo on TV.

"She's kind of a local celebrity. She does all kinds of shows about things going on in Chicago." Mom's voice came out uncharacteristically monotone. Her eyes were glued to the screen.

I sat back and watched as models paraded in front of the camera, flipped open fur coats, flashed rings and smiled for the studio audience. At almost the same time I thought about turning up the volume, we were summoned into I.C.U. and shuffled from the waiting room to Dad's side.

Don't ever have a heart attack. If your heart stopping doesn't kill you, you'll kill yourself weeks after you leave the hospital, once you realize how terrible you looked while you were unconscious in the ICU. Dad was one of the lucky ones--he had no hair, so bed head was off the table. But he still looked pasty and the tubes running out of his mouth, nose and hands didn't do anything to enhance his odds at "50 Most Handsome Men" either. Nurses came in, gliding silently along on rubber-soled shoes while pulling plugs, loosening tubes and lowering bed rails.

"What's going on?" I asked. I knew he was alive by the annoying high-pitched beeping of the heart machine, so they couldn't be prepping him for a trip to the morgue.

"He's being transferred," a young woman whispered in a crisp, soft voice as if the conversation would wake my father.

"What for?" Mom asked.

The nurse avoided eye contact and continued fussing around my father's side. "You'll have to talk to the doctor."

***

That infamous summer Oprah entered our lives, I lived in a remodeled garage in Los Angeles' San Fernando Valley. I hated the sun, heat and dryness of the Valley, but I had been in Southern California for a couple of years and built myself what passed for a life--albeit not a pathetic one. The phone rang one morning about 7 a.m. It was my mother. I hadn't spoken with her very often since that day at the kitchen table when we looked at photographs, when she asked me to "give her and Dad time" and I agreed. I had given them lots of time. A couple years worth of time, in fact. During that time, I had heard nothing. So that morning when I heard her voice, thick with tears, choking, I knew it wasn't a call to reconnect and end our estrangement. I knew it was something serious.

"David," she said, "it's . . ." She never finished that sentence. Instead, there was a shuffle and her voice was replaced by my sister who did the same thing, shuffling the phone to someone else.

"It's your dad," a male voice on the phone said to me. He was the neighbor who lived behind us during my childhood; a cheery fellow with a wicked sense of humor and mischievous twinkle in his eyes. "They don't know if he'll live through the day. He could go at anytime."

I felt nothing when I heard this. It resonated with the strength of hearing about the death of someone you don't know--a random face on a random newspaper headline.

"Then call me when he dies," I said and hung up. I figured why waste the money of flying out to Chicago now? Much better to save the money for when he actually goes. Then I wouldn't have to waste two flights.

I told a friend about my decision and her response was "It doesn't matter how angry you are at a parent. If you don't see them before they die you'll regret it forever." I have no idea why I took this advice, but I did. I was on the next plane to Chicago, my estranged parents, and Oprah.

***

Dad was transferred because he needed a surgical procedure which was only done at the hospital in Elgin. The next day, when I arrived at the ICU, Mom sat watching Oprah again. This time Oprah was interviewing some people who I didn't recognize.

"Oh, they're some Chicago politicians." Mom explained.

"I thought she did fluff pieces with furs and stuff."

"That was yesterday," Mom nodded. "She does all kinds of stuff."

I nodded and sat back to wait for the doctors to arrive and let Oprah teach me about Chicago politics.

Thus began our relationship with Oprah. For the next several days, we would filter into the waiting room, watch Oprah and wait for the next development with my dad. Oprah became an odd touchstone to our lives; a way for us to be together without really communicating, keep up the illusion that we weren't worrying about what the future held, nor why we had gone so long without speaking. We slid into a silent understanding that we needed to be at the ICU waiting room well in advance of the Oprah Show so we could grab the hard, plastic chairs that had a clear view of the TV and not the hard, plastic chairs that forced you to crane your neck to see the screen. We brought our coffee or hot chocolate, our snacks and our strung-out, thinning patience. We would sit glued to Oprah, only talking during commercial breaks. Oprah got us through those harried first days of anxious waiting, armed only with her smile, raucous personality and hair.

***

The night before Dad's angioplasty, I sat with Mom at the kitchen table and made small talk while she chain smoked. When we had exhausted the weather, the quality of food in the hospital and other issues of avoidance, she turned to me and said, "Thanks for coming."

That one comment grated on my nerves like nails on a chalkboard. After all this time, energy and frustration, a "thanks" is all I get? I turned to her and said, "I didn't want to."

She began to cry, "What do you mean?"

"I haven't heard from you for all this time and suddenly I'm supposed to care?"

"We're your family."

I remember stammering, "All those years I heard 'You're our son' and 'You're part of this family'--then, when you find out I'm gay you dump me? What's that about?"

"You need to understand--" she began. I never let her finish that statement, a moment that seared itself into my brain. For years, I've wondered what followed that statement. But that's one train that will never return to the station--kind of like a TV movie where you missed the ending, but never gets released on DVD, so you'll never find out the ending.

Words began to spew from me uncontrollably, so fast I can't remember if I made English sentences or if I ran them together like a tape on fast forward.

"People throw those words around, like 'family' and 'love' and what the hell does that mean, anyway? Don't people who love each other accept them for who they are? What about those mothers that go on TV talking about how much they love their son who just murdered an entire family?"

"What the hell are you talking about?" Mom really didn't understand.

"About the hypocrisy of it all. Like 'You're our family as long as you do what we like'. Actions speak louder than words. Or silence.

Jesus, Ma, family doesn't ditch someone like an unwanted friend at the mall."

Throughout my venomous monologue, Mom watched me and nodded.

"I've been alone, Ma. I really needed advice. I needed help."

"You're doing fine."

"How the hell would you know?" I felt warm, like standing beside a furnace. "I'm terrified! I hate my job, I hate my life, I have no idea what the hell I'm doing in life. I can use some help here and there's nobody I can trust to help."

"That's not true."

"How do you know?" I asked again. "You don't know anything about me."

Mom stopped crying and turned on me. Her eyes were suddenly dry and her face stern. "Who's fault is that? You never told us anything. You want help and advice? Ask for it. You want us to support you? Then share. I can't help you if I don't know there's a problem."

"Like you would have been there, right?" I didn't know if I sounded sarcastic, but I wanted to. Where's the reality show TV crew when you need them?

"You'll never know, will you?"

What do you say to that? All was quiet for a moment, until at last she said, "We need to start again. Just . . . start over."

"Fine," I shot back. "Then you need to accept you have a gay son. If you invite me to see you, I may bring a guy. I have a life-- okay, not a good one--but it's mine and you have no control with what I'm doing with it. It's got to be on different terms, Ma."

She sucked on her cigarette and I watched the smoke flow out of her mouth, sending a puffy cloud into the air. We sat in silence until she finally said, "Everything is going to be different now."

"We'll see," I said.

After another long pause she added, "Maybe we'll come see you in Los Angeles. I've never been to Southern California. I'd like to go."

"Then come on," I said.

Then we returned to sitting in silence, her cigarette sitting in the ashtray burning silently.

***

Mom brought me out of my reverie when she said, "Oprah has really changed over the years, you know?"

"Yeah," I agreed. "I know."

"I like her," Mom said, turning up the volume.

"Me, too."

The Dock

"This was your father's favorite part of the house, really," Mom said as I followed her down the slope of the backyard to the small dock Dad had built on the shore of the modest-sized lake. "He sat down on this dock for hours. He always wanted me to join him down here, but my God! How boring is it to sit and look at water all day? That is just not my deal."

Dad sat on this dock to contemplate his navel, watch the Canada geese, or god-knows what else early-rising people do during the pre-dawn hours of the day. Often I would wake and stand at the sliding glass door in the kitchen with a mug of coffee watching him sitting on the ancient metal lawn chair watching the morning stillness. I never did understand what he was looking at. I never bothered watching water for more than a couple minutes. Yes, watching the water calms the nerves and I've heard that it inspires poets. But, seriously, water's water. What's it going to do? Stand up and roll over? Leap up and do somersaults? It's water, for crying out loud, not a spaniel. Bodies of water are fickle. They lay there, acting peaceful and serene as long as you stand on the shore admiring them from afar. But the minute you dive under the surface for a swim, the temperamental-bitch personality kicks in and she drags you under the waves and tries to drowns you. My grandfather taught me well.

Dad loved watching bodies of water, though, regardless of size. He felt a special connection with this water behind the house. He'd get in his beloved miniature electric-motor-powered boat and circle the lake; sometimes cutting the engine in the middle of the lake and drifting aimlessly, lost in thought. I could understand his fascination with the small lake if he and Mom were in the habit of leaping off the dock into the water with adolescent glee; or challenged each other to friendly skinny-dipping races, or taking romantic canoe rides around its perimeter beneath a moonlit sky on a summer's night. I could excuse his obsession with the lake if he was a Flower Child from the '60s reliving acid trips, but as far as I know, the only thing he knew about drugs was that they came in smart packaging and made guest appearances on *Law and Order*. That, and Mom visited a hash bar while vacationing in Europe. Besides, Mom didn't even like being in the boat. So I chalked this water-watching phase up to him being weird. Or retired.

I turned to Mom, who stood next to me in the backyard looking at the dock. It was a simple, functional piece of work; jutting out 12 feet into the water, the L-shaped wooden pier was home to Dad's small electrically-motored boat as well as a variety of mismatched lawn chairs. Here, then, was the centerpiece of his life after he and Mom retired, and the last remnant of his to be cleaned up after his funeral. And cleaning up was putting it lightly; judging by the masses of wires and switches attached to the wooden structure, Dad had been tinkering out here as much as the basement. "Jerry rigging" he called it. "Messing with stuff until it broke" was my term. Dad's favorite saying was "jerry rigging"--a turn of phrase I couldn't find in the dictionary and wondered where the hell it came from. When I was very small, I asked Mom one day what it meant.

"It's not jerry-rigging!" Mom would snap back. "It's good 'ol Yankee ingenuity!"

There you go. (For the record--later research revealed the origin of the phrase is "jerry-built". I guess neither the word *built* nor the hyphen were considered good enough to stay in the English language.)

The dock wasn't immune to the forces of Dad's wild improvisation. On the left side of the L stood one of those cheap white plastic garden cabinets you see in the glossy ads which are jammed into the Sunday newspaper--the ones that spill out of the center of the paper and pile up on the floor as you reach across the kitchen table for more coffee. The cabinet looked so innocently midwestern as it basked in the sunshine on this warm spring day--it stood about five feet tall, three feet wide and its inside sported three shelves. Its outer cabinet doors, when closed, provided a small ring through which one could secure a padlock. It was the kind of cabinet unit that you find on sale at Lowe's for less than the cost of the gas to haul the thing home. It was held together with interlocking pieces (No tools necessary! Just snap the easy to assemble pieces together and instantly store your garden supplies!). I opened the unlocked doors and out tumbled some fishing nets, a tangled mess of fishing line, bobbers, a life vest and a slew of miscellaneous stuff that Dad kept as treasures, but the rest of us relinquish to trash dumps.

"It's old and full of spider webs," Mom declared, pointing at the plastic shed. "Just take it down. I'd do it myself, but my I don't have the strength to haul it away."

"You're sure you don't want to keep it?"

"For what? More crap? Don't I have enough crap around here?"

No comment.

"All right. Consider the thing gone," I assured her. How hard could this be? Advertisers like to use words like "durable" and "sturdy" but we all know that is adspeak for "It's manufactured by low-paid Chinese workers with sub-standard materials, so you're buying a piece of cheap crap that's a step above cardboard." I bought a similar piece of crap when I lived in Maine. Every time I touched it, the thing would fall apart into a heap on the basement floor. I took Dad's lead and tried jerry-rigging it with duct tape, wrapping wire around the joints, leaning it against the basement wall, praying to pagan gods and whatever else I could think of, to no avail. Last time I saw it, it sagged against the dumpster behind my townhouse and a stray cat had taken up residence on the bottom shelf.

All things considered, there was plenty of time to yank Dad's cheap, plastic shelf unit into a pile and haul it to the dump before noon. Then we could take off for an early lunch, then maybe to the movies. If I used my Son Look, I could probably get Mom to spring for the popcorn.

I grabbed the large white thing by the sides and pulled, thinking I would haul the whole unit as one piece to the truck, saving myself the bother of disassembling it and making several trips. It didn't budge under the force. It felt as if I pulled on a rock; solid and unyielding.

"When did Dad get this?" I asked Mom, suspecting that Dad must have bolted it to the dock. Damn. This would mean finding the right socket wrench, undoing the bolts and making the several trips I was trying to avoid. There would be no "early" to the lunch.

"Oh, a couple years ago," she said. "It took him about five minutes to put it together. It's a cheap piece of shit. Besides, you know how he loved to tinker with shit."

I grabbed the door of the cabinet, knowing it was only attached to the roof section and the floor section at either end by a finger of plastic that fits neatly inside the hole of the upper shelf unit. Like the story goes, "Insert slot A into hole B". Nothing wrong here folks, just a minor set-back. I pulled. It fought back. I yanked. It didn't care. No matter how much I tugged, the door's fingers of plastic remained firmly rooted in the base at both the top and bottom. Screw it, I thought, there were two doors, so I tried the second door. It, too, refused to budge.

I grabbed a hammer and shoved the claw end into the narrow gap between the door and the main unit. The door buckled but didn't snap.

"Ma, come here and hold the door, okay?" She did and I applied more pressure to the hinge side of the door. No good. I moved back to the first door. Same results. Soon we had a cheap molded plastic storage shed that looked like it had grown breasts.

"Reach under the doors and pull." Mom said.

I did. With a loud CRACK the upper finger of the left door popped out of the hole.

"Damn! This thing is a pistol!" Mom said.

"Did he super glue this thing together?" I asked, looking at the deformed door and deciding that if I ever a offered a superpower, screw things like *flight* and *telepathy*--I'm going for *ability to blow up stuff*. First on my list: this freakin' plastic storage shed. "Now, we just pull the bottom of the door from slot B and we've got it." I grabbed the door and pulled upwards. Then I screamed as the plastic remnants sliced through my finger and blood gushed out into the water. The damn thing just bit me! The door remained fully entrenched in slot B.

"Don't kill yourself, for God's sake!" Mom chastised me.

"God-damn!" I kicked at the cheap plastic door in exasperation. It swung away from me and hung limply over the water; beaten but still kicking. "What do we have to do to this thing? Set the frickin' pier on fire and melt it?"

"Well, it gets a lot of weather out here: rain, ice, snow . . ."

"So do postal carriers but they're not indestructible!"

"Your dad wanted it to stay put, I guess."

"Staying put is one thing; fusing it to the dock is something else! So he took this cheap piece of crap plastic and what? Morphed it into concrete?"

The door clung to the plastic storage shed with all the gusto of Mel Gibson's character in *Braveheart* when he lay strung out on a table getting his penis chopped off by the British. It knew it was doomed, but it planned to make me work for my victory. I grabbed the plastic with a renewed vigor and sense of determination. It's a finger of plastic shoved into a hole, for god's sake! I was a human being with a Master's degree! I had a brain. I had opposable thumbs. This shed was an inanimate object that didn't even have hands. There was no way it was going to defeat me. After five minutes of tugging, pulling, swearing, and throwing myself at it like a five-year-old throwing a tantrum, the door finally gave up and broke free with a loud CRACK. I chucked it onto the dock with a grunt of frustration and threw my arms up in the air in triumph.

"We win!" I screamed, wiping the sweat off my face.

"Congratulations," Mom said, "You beat the shit out of a hunk of plastic." Mom picked up the remnants of the door and inspected it carefully.

"There's no glue on this!" Mom said.

"Yeah, Mom, I noticed that."

"That should have been easy to take apart. It's just a bit of plastic in a hole."

"You're right, Ma. I've been playing around because I have nothing better to do than hammer a piece of plastic."

"Don't be a sarcastic shit," Mom snapped, analyzing the end of the door. "Wow. That's strange. What's holding it in place?"

"No idea, Ma."

One door down. One door, three sides and a roof of the crappy piece of plastic to go. I look at the time and realize it's been almost 20 minutes and we've removed one door. At this rate, we may wrap it up just before sunset. We are definitely NOT going out to lunch. Maybe there'll be time for the movie, though.

This time, it's war. I stare down the second door and strategize my plan of attack. I grab the claw hammer and spin it in my palm, analyzing the shed for its Achilles heel. Then I see it: A small gap between the wooden dock and the underside of the remaining door. I estimate there is just enough space to accommodate the claw of the hammer, allowing for enough leverage to propel the bottom loose from the wood. I take a deep breath and throw myself onto the dock. I hurl myself into the handle of the hammer, shoving the claw between the opening and the wood. I whirl around, bracing my feet on the inside of the back wall and tighten my grip on the tool. I simultaneously pull on the hammer and thrust with both my legs, sending all my force into the cheap, plastic wall. The shed groans with agony as the nails holding the floor to the dock are wrenched from the wood. Then, with a heavy THUD, it keels backward onto the deck and lies still. It is dead. I have beaten the plastic shed.

"Now the roof," Mom declared, "then the walls should be easy. They'll fall like a house of cards."

"No sweat," I said. This time, I'm ready for the sucker. I declare a full assault on the plastic shed by hammering upwards against the roof section from inside.

"Well, I'll be," Mom said. "That's really stuck in there, isn't it?"

"Yeah," I groaned. Sweat dripping into my eyes, I dropped the hammer onto the dock and picked up my secret weapon.

"What are you going to do with a hack saw?" Mom asked.

"Go Jeffrey Dahmer on it!" Note to self: Worry when you begin to identify with serial killers. I placed the blade about half way up the side and began sawing. This time, we'll just cut the damn thing down the middle, yank the top half off and screw trying to disassemble bit by bit. I'm totally going to draw and quarter this sucker. Ten minutes later, I hacked into the sides about an inch. Goddammit! About forty minutes had gone by and we'd gotten two doors off.

"You did better when you were kicking the hell out of it," Mom said. She was right. I began kicking it. It didn't help.

"I cannot believe this!" I threw myself at it in frustration. "How in the hell did he put this together?" I went Hulk against the cheap plastic, yanking, pulling, kicking and screaming.

"Jesus Christ, where did you learn language like that?"

"You and Dad."

"Maybe from your dad, but not from me," Mom snorted. "Here, I'll help."

She pulled on the unit. I shoved the crowbar underneath the bottom shelf while throwing myself against it. A loud CRACK echoed over the lake and the shed flopped onto Mom, who caught it like a pro linebacker. All that was left now was four huge, rusty bolts drilled through the wood of the dock with jagged pieces of white plastic sticking out from under the rusty washers.

"Damn!" I said, pointing. "Here's the reason! Dad bolted the sucker to the dock with four bolts."

"Look at the size of them!" Mom shrugged. "I guess he wanted to make sure it didn't go anywhere."

"These bolts are the size of Detroit. What the hell was he expecting? A hurricane?"

I adjusted the wrench and started unscrewing the bolts. They were tight from the rust that had accumulated around the threads. I tugged on the wrench. They stayed. I smacked them with the flat side of the tool. They remained motionless.

"I'm going to need vice grips," I snapped at Mom. She fingered the tools lined up on the dock.

"These?" She said, holding out the vice grips. I snatched them from her. "Yes."

After another five minutes of swearing, tugging and beating the first bit of metal gave up its valiant struggle and spun free.

"Finally!" I said.

"Well," Mom agreed, "that's one."

The second and third were the same. Finally, I pulled the third one from the wood of the dock. As I lifted it out of the hole, a tiny splash rang out.

"What was that?" Mom asked.

"I think it was a washer Dad placed on the underside of the bolt." I guessed. "How in the crap did he get a washer UNDER the dock? Did he go into the lake?"

"Maybe he had one of the grandkids helping him. They liked getting into the water."

The final bolt spun wildly, giving me no resistance.

"Crap," I said, throwing down the wrench and falling onto my back on the dock. "It's stripped. Now the freaking thing will never come out."

Mom leaned over, grabbed the bolt in her fingers and pulled. The bolt slipped out with ease. She stood over me with the rusty hunk of metal in her hand. "This one wasn't even fastened down."

"Which means there were three bolts holding that bloody thing onto the dock," I sighed. "That's impossible. It felt like the whole cabinet was cemented in place."

Mom wasn't listening. She was already putting her Obsessive Compulsive Disorder to good use by cleaning up the fragments of plastic, the discarded bolts and various tools. When the dock was nothing but a L-shaped hunk of weathered wood jutting into the lake, she motioned for me to follow her up to the house.

"Let's go have some lunch," she said, leading the way. "It's almost noon. I don't think we'll get to the matinee."

"Dad should have gone into construction."

"He loved this dock," Mom said, barely a whisper. "If he had his way, he never would have come in off the lake."

Even after death he didn't want to come in off the lake. Knowing Dad, he's already at work planning some divine revenge against us because we tore down the last vestige of his safe haven. A vengeful father haunting us from the great beyond. Great. As a kid, I dreamed of my life being a great Jules Verne adventure, what I'm getting is a great Shakespearean tragedy.

JUNE, 2009
Catching the Wild Wave

"Want to go tubing?" Mom asked.

"Tubing?"

"You know, you get in a huge inner tube and float down a river." I can hear the sarcasm dripping from her voice, even though the cell phone makes her sound distant and a bit . . . flimsy. But in all fairness, she's got a PhD in sarcasm.

"I know what tubing is, Mom."

What I didn't know is into which river she planned to throw her sixty-five year old retired body. Recently a friend of mine took her boyfriend to Wyoming and did some tubing in the Rockies, where MOUNTAINS and WATER make OPPORTUNITIES FOR TUBING. Mom lives in Tennessee, halfway between Knoxville and Nashville. The only river they had was that one the four guys transversed in *Deliverance*. Like I learned from Kentucky natives when I went to graduate school in Lexington: "The only thing worse than being from Kentucky is being from Tennessee." There's nothing much of interest in Tennessee, besides Nashville and--let's face it--in the twenty-first century, even Nashville has lost its glamour. Most of the recordings come out of New York and Los Angeles anyway. The Grand Ole Opry may have been genuine country in its day, but in 2009, it is one step away from an entertainment theme park. One of the reasons Dad wanted to live in that house where Mom was now living alone was due to the fact that you have to drive a half-hour to find a stop light. Dad liked to be alone. He's the one person I know who wanted to trade places with Robinson Crusoe.

"It's fun," she said, bringing me out of my daze.

"You went tubing already?"

She said, "I went with your sister when she took the kids. It's a blast."

"Yes," I said, determined not to be outdone by my sister, "I want to go tubing. When?"

Sibling rivalry: the roller coaster than never stops. I always thought adolescent jealousy would fade when my sister and I grew up, got jobs, started lives of our own and got partners. But here I am, years later, still harboring that lingering suspicion that maybe she is doing better than I. Maybe somehow she has become more mature, more financially viable or more emotionally stable. At least in my old age I've discovered I'm not alone--who doesn't feel that way? Be honest. Can't you hear yourself saying, "Well, I got fired again, split with the meathead and I'm on probation, but my sister/brother forgot Mom's birthday. Life is SO gonna suck for them." Break-ups and layoffs get sympathy. Forgetting to send flowers on a birthday gets the Mom Look.

There was no way my sister was going to come out looking more fun, hip and spontaneous than me. Damn her and her river-riding/inner-tubing excursion. Any fun she can have, I can have funner.

This was war.

***

Apparently the days of uneducated, cousin-marrying hillbillies who are genetically allergic to dentists are over. Tennessee has dragged itself into the modern age. They have joined the every increasing ranks of "states where you can go inner-tubing."

Who knew?

Upon hearing of my sister's inner-tube adventure on the river with her kids, Mom hit the web to see if the place my sister recommended had a website. She found several websites of several businesses. Then, Mom found the links to the pictures that showed the river's locations. From that, she veered into the Tennessee Parks and Recreation Department website, the state of the riverways of Tennessee, and God knows what else her retired self was able to uncover. Seemingly overnight, she transformed from Mom the "Oh, I only use it for email" confused senior citizen into Neo from *The Matrix*. I have visions of her holing up in the back bedroom of the house with a stack of Hot Pockets and a mini-fridge so she wouldn't have to leave the computer room for her meals. Apparently, she had visions of the red pill.

Thus, several weeks later I found myself clinging to a yellow donut of a balloon drifting on a slow-moving Tennessee waterway. The fun never stops, does it?

The current brought me to the edge of the river, where deep black mud met the clear water. From this angle, I could see the exposed roots of the trees as they clung to the side of the embankment, peaking through the dark soil like children spying on the Christmas tree.

I spun myself around so I could kick away from the bank and felt myself inching towards the center of the waterway, where I could see the leaves barreling along the surface of the water, like tiny battle cruisers headed toward some fierce enemy. It was only when I pulled my gaze away from the leaves and took in the surface of the river did I notice EVERYTHING was clicking along faster than I was--leaves, twigs and other natural refuse. Great. Now I'm officially slower than a floating twig.

I caught sight of my mother. She had somehow managed to reach the center of the current, despite the fact that she left the launching area after I did. She folded herself into the middle of the giant yellow donut, with her butt hanging into the water while her arms and legs flowed over the sides of the tube. She flailed her hands, but only her fingertips reached the water, barely touching the surface. She kicked furiously, sending her yellow donut bobbing up and down, her toes narrowly missing the river. She looked like a spastic turtle turned on its back.

She was talking to my niece, who hovered a few feet away inside her own giant donut. Her face lit up, not only because she caked herself with sunblock and set about seeking the sun like a deranged camel, but with happiness. I couldn't hear the exact words, but I did hear . . . "fun".

About twenty minutes later, I had somehow gotten my bright yellow tube to inch over into the center of the water and I kicked and paddled myself close to Mom.

"Having fun yet?"

She nodded. "Too bad we didn't know about this place a long time ago," she said as the sound of what could be rapids neared. "Your dad would have loved it."

***

It feels like an hour later and I'm trapped between two rocks. Again. The sun is frying my semi-bald head. Again. There are those that flock to the sand and heat of Phoenix, Las Vegas and Albuquerque so they can throw themselves onto a lounge chair, coat themselves with oil and lie in the sun.

My line of thinking: MEAT + OIL + HEAT = BBQ

The sun is meant to be used as a source of power and one day it will be, once we figure out how to make money off solar power. Other than that, sunlight needs to remain the domain of chlorophyll.

I am not a sun person; I am a night person.

"You like to live in caves," my friend, Holly, would tell me. "Do you ever rent an apartment with a window?"

"God, I hope not," I would respond. "Then those evil rays of the sun will melt me." I'm the opposite of the Wicked Witch of the West.

It was a running joke. You had to be there.

I look to my left and see that a few feet away, in the widest part of the river, several youngsters frolicked in the water, basking under the glorious shade of the trees lining the shore. Floating nearby are their yellow inner tubes: waterlogged donuts set free to swim their way home. The children laugh, scream, and speak in excited German, making them sound like a Heineken commercial on crack.

I should feel happy for them, but the more I watch them, the more I really want a bratwurst and a beer.

I struggle against the confines of my yellow donut and try to reach the sides of the river with my foot so I can propel myself out into the middle of the water and drop off this floating whoopie cushion. I want to be in the water; I want to submerge myself in the coolness of the river and escape this scorching heat. Some people like the surface. I like to dive underneath.

Mom, who was behind me for several minutes, floats carelessly on the current and is brought crashing into the throng of Germans, where she joins in with their laughter, pointing and joking as if she could speak the language. What is it with her and Germans, by the way? The woman can walk down the street in the wilds of the Amazon jungle and stumble upon a German candy store.

I want to be over there with her, not here along the banks struggling to break free of the rocks from hell. I want to be floating freely and not trapped.

But, that's me: I always want to be somewhere else than where I am.

I'm sure this revelation is going to be important in my life somehow, but right now, I just want out of the damn sun! I roll off the yellow donut, barely missing the part of the rock hidden beneath the surface, and swim out to join the throng of glee-filled Germans and my mother, who by now has become a victim of their splash wars. By the time I drag myself and the yellow donut over to them, the joke is over and the crowd dispersing. The sun has even shifted. I'm now behind my mother standing in the sun. She waves. I wave back and haul myself onto the tube. Maybe if I follow her, I can wind up in a herd of Germans laughing about something I can't understand.

The water ahead begins to pick up speed and downstream I see the white movement of water over rocks. "Rapids" would be exaggerating--when I think of "rapids", I think of Meryl Streep strapped into a boat fleeing Kevin Bacon in *The River Wild*. What sits ahead of me is the Tennessee version of rapids. I call them "Rapids Lite"--same great picture, half the thrills.

My tube snags on a rock (again) and when the current pulls it loose, I go spinning counter-clockwise down the river a few feet only to hit a rock hidden just under the surface, and repeat the process spinning in the opposite direction. As I flail in the water to spin my inner-tube around so I can face the final leg of the one-mile trip head-on, I spot a cluster of rocks in the middle of the river a few yards away, forming another set of rapids-lite. There's a woman standing amongst the white upsurge, her eyes squinted against the sun, flailing at the pathetic excuse for waves, as if she's never had a bath before. I notice two things about this situation immediately: 1) the woman stands in water that is waist high, meaning she is really, REALLY tall, or the water is really, REALLY shallow and, 2) she has no inner tube. An inner-tubeless person on an inner-tubing expedition instantly alerts me to the fact that all is not well in inner-tubing land.

I paddle my way towards her with all the grace of an obese, paraplegic turtle.

"I fell off my tube," she says with disgust. "I hurt my leg." She awkwardly lifts her leg against the current of the river and shows me the blood pouring out of the cut on her calf.

"Looks nasty. Where's your tube?" I ask, steadying myself on one of the rocks that compose rapids-lite. She points a few feet away. I see a yellow "O" beached on another rock not too far away, where it lays sunning itself. Great. Even the stupid inner tubes are Sun Lovers. Damn them. I slide off my tube and hand it to her.

"Get in this, I'll go fetch yours."

"I need help getting in it," she whines. What do I look like? The freaking Coast Guard?

I grab her arm and we struggle against the suddenly strong current to lift her into the tube, but the flow pushes her backwards, onto me. I'm just about ready to verbally bitch-slap this woman for being unable to withstand water moving half-mile an hour when, thankfully, a stray kayak floats along with a teenage boy in it. He lodges himself on the rocks and takes her other arm so together, we get the bleeding, possibly weak-due-to-anemia woman into the yellow donut and give her a shove. She is off and floating.

I turn to the beached inner-tube she has abandoned and wade towards it. Suddenly, my foot lands on an underwater rock and I slip on the slime. Under the water I go. A pain shoots through my leg and I can feel my feet trapped under something large . . . something hard, yet squishy. I can't tell if its a piece of river junk or a log. Either way, I really don't want to see it, so I pull myself free, inch towards the beached inner-tube just as a swirl of water from rapids-lite frees it, sending the yellow donut shooting downstream.

The fun never stops when you're inner-tubing.

Just then, I spot an orphaned yellow donut creeping towards me on the surface of the water. Some other poor sod's misfortune is just what I need to get me on my way. What luck! Serendipity happens so rarely in my life, I'll take what I can get.

At the end of the one-mile route, the thoughtful workers of the yellow donut rental facility have hung a huge sign announcing the end of the fun-filled, action-packed ride and instructing all those thrill seekers renting yellow donuts to haul their sun-baked behinds out of the donut hole and walk up the path to the bus-loading zone. Although Mom and I didn't make an exit strategy for the river tube, I leap to the conclusion that I ought to wait for her here. To my delight, the ramp leading to the bus loading zone is in the shade, so I hunker down on a large rock and wait, examining my bleeding leg.

About ten minutes later, I'm beginning to wonder where she is. Both she and my niece shot past me while I was hauling Ms. Whiner into her tube. Even though they haven't passed by, there is no other exit off the river, and any reasonable person can deduce that in a few moments they'll be making their appearance, I begin to worry. Did their donut spring a leak, pulling them down into the four-foot-deep water of the slow moving river? What if they were ambushed by a crowd of yellow inner tube maniacs, forced off the rubber floatation devices and left to their own devices amongst strangers? Perhaps they've been caught by the donut police, eager to make off with a new mascot for their coffee breaks. How is it possible I've taken her from New York to Europe with no mishap, yet here in the backwater of Tennessee she meets her demise? What would Dad think? He spent an enormous amount of time telling me I had to take care of her and not let anything befall her and I let him down. Done in by a trickle of water whose greatest claim to fame is hauling hillbillies from point A to point B. He was right. I am going to get her killed.

Suddenly I see Mom and my niece coming around the bend, oblivious of the fact that they were headed straight for Rotten Rapids-lite. Odd--from this distance, Rotten Rapids-lite looks like the river ride's version of the Dumbo ride at Disneyland. How in the hell did I manage to loose my donut, slice my shin open and get run over by a chain smoker? Mom and my niece are holding hands; looking like conjoined twins with giant yellow donut butts. They are laughing. They sail over the Rotten Rapids-lite with barely a bob. They emerge dry and un-bleeding. For a moment I hate them and their naive luck.

"What the hell happened to you?" Mom asks, pointing to my leg as she approaches the exit ramp.

"I was attacked by those stupid rocks while trying to help a woman back into her freakin' bloody donut."

"Well, that wasn't too smart."

"Well, it's not like I planned it to happen," I spew venomously. "It's not like I didn't have anything else to do. Besides, where were you?"

"On the river."

"You were gone forever. I thought you drowned, or fell off the tube or something."

Mom shakes her head and gestures to my niece, giving her the sign for CRAZY as she points at me. "You worry too much, dear."

I grab both Mom's tube and mine and stagger up the cement steps that extend from the river's edge to the narrow, unpaved road on the ledge above. I want to feel like I worry too much, too, but I don't. Instead, I launch into a tirade of justification of my overprotective nature by telling her about my floating experience; the repeated entrapment between tree roots and embankment, the struggling to maintain a shred of dignity while doing the Turtle Paddle towards the current and the constant battle against the hot sun. I show her the gash on my leg, the bruised shin and the sunburn that is making my shoulder sting. I tell her that she should be more thankful to me because tubing can be hazardous to her health and I'm trying to look after her.

Just as I finish, I suddenly hear Dad's voice in my head, "If anything happens to her, I'm going to blame you." Jeesh. Aren't voices from the Great Beyond supposed to whisper words of support and encouragement? Even while sitting in his recliner in the sky, with the opportunity to watch any ball game he wants without paying the Pay Per View price, he chooses to watch us float on a donut.

"It was a rough ride!" I say finally.

"Just like your life--you always do things the hard way," she snapped. "I'm easy. I'm not cheap, but I'm easy!" My niece laughs at this and I glower at her. I expected Mom to say something like, "My, David, what a terrible bruise that is!" or "Holy cow! That is a nasty gash on your shin!" Instead, she follows that up with "Jesus Christ, David. It's a freaking RIVER! Where was I going to go? Timbuktu?"

I shrug. What else can I do? She's right. I worry too much. I blame Dad, since, being dead, he can't defend himself and I finally get the last word.

"I just like to sit back and go where the river takes me," Mom says as we wait for the shuttle to return us to the inner tube shop. "The river only flows one way, why fight it?"

Next time, I'll just mope and brood, as it makes me feel better.

PHOTOS

"You keep everything?" I asked Mom, looking at the box of photos she has placed on the dining room table. She nods although I know the answer and she knows I know the answer. It was said more as a rhetorical question. Mom and Dad both saved everything. Mom has always been the less cluttered of the two, but even she is about two steps away from a guest appearance on *Hoarders*. She has crammed the lake house's basement full of everything, ranging from last year's birthday gift boxes ("You'll never know when you may need a box!") to scraps of ribbons and bows from the Christmas party when Mary and Joseph hosted ("It was half off!"). Mom has an oblong, plastic storage box dedicated to Christmas wrapping paper, purchased on December 26th of last year, during the "After Christmas Clearance Sale". I told you: she can smell a sale like wolves smell fear. Growing up, we were the only kids I knew that opened Christmas gifts with a knife next to us, so if we got a gift in a box, we could cut the tape instead of tearing into the box. Back then, it was embarrassing. It was called "cheap". Now, it's popular. It's called "going green". My family always was ahead of its time.

"Now I don't have to buy wrapping paper next year," Mom would explain every year as we hauled the lightly flattened roles of wrapping paper into the garage. "Nobody's going to care if it is out of style. Cute Santa bears this year look just like cute Santa bears last year." Dad shared Mom's lust for collecting stuff, only he was better at holding on to useless items. Where Mom could explain why she still had two year old bubble wrap, Dad had no idea what the gadget in the box in the corner was; he only knew it looked cool and he had used it once in 1962 and proved useful.

I had just entered the garage, where Dad had built himself a workbench which ran the entire length of the structure. He always said it was for him to keep his tools organized. True, he did have an envious assortment of Craftsman tools dangling from wires and S-hooks on the pegboard. It was also true that he had dozens of baby food jars filled with washers, nuts, bolts, assorted nails and pieces of metal alongside of bits of wire scavenged from the Lawn Department of K-Mart, a ball of twine the size of Pittsburgh that he had "acquired" from the loading dock at his work, and an endless pile of plastic twist ties for plastic garbage bags that never seemed to hold the top of garbage bags closed, but did an impressive job of providing enough ballast to hold the bench onto the floor of the garage.

As I kid, I often sat on the floor of the living room in front of our brand-new COLOR (!!) television, praying my parents would be chosen as contestants on *Let's Make a Deal*. They're the only people I know that when asked if they had a 1955 nickel, could come up with one. Our family was just one game show away from a lifetime supply of Rice-A-Roni. The downside to their obsessive collecting was that I could never find anything, either in the house or the garage. The upside to this is that I feel safe knowing when Western Civilization as we know it goes spiraling downward out of control, and people find themselves living a *Mad Max* film, my parents are on my team. They may not know the antidote to radiation poisoning, but we'd always have plenty of gift wrapping paper and twist ties.

Ironically, just before I left Dad's workbench to join Mom inside the house and caught her at the table going through old photos, I had just been staring at Dad's treasured tools. I had just been wondering how we were going to dispose of all his stuff. Mom had told me that morning she had decided to give most of the tools to my brother-in-law.

"All I ever use is a hammer and screwdriver," she explained. "The stuff should go to someone who will use it. What's the use of a tool if it just hangs there? Tools need to be used." This flashback sat heavy on my heart. I realized I was probably like most people in the world--not seeing my parents for who they were, per se, but the things they said, stuff they collected and behaviors they demonstrated. Our parents aren't so much people but character traits.

"You always laugh at me for keeping stuff, but aren't you glad I kept these?" Mom jolts me out of the mental wheel-spinning as she reaches into the box of pictures and grabs a handful, which she hands to me. "God, I didn't know we had so many pictures."

Neither did I. My family wasn't much for photos while I was growing up. Only years later, when my sister and I had left home did Mom and Dad embrace the fine art of haphazard photography. The addiction started when Dad bought a video camera one year and began to document everything they did with the meticulousness of a National Geographic mini-series. One time I asked Dad why he felt the need to film everything.

"So we can watch the videos and remember the trip."

"So you and Mom are going to sit down one day, pop in a VHS and watch 47 hours of your cruise through the Panama Canal with the senior citizen brigade?"

"You never know," Dad told me. "And don't be a sarcastic shit. I like remembering the trips your mom and I take together."

"But you have the memories. Why do you need the VHS tapes?"

He sighed and shook his head. "The cable may go out for a really long time."

Apparently the cable never went out long enough, for soon after that conversation, Dad bought Mom a digital camera for her birthday and she was off and running with this new toy, snapping still frames of real life with the zest of a person who forgot they HAVE a real life to live. The VHS camera went the way of the Gameboy that I gave to Dad one Christmas and found years later still in its box.

"These are all the trips your Dad and I took," she said, flipping through the photographs. "I want to do something with them."

I took a stack of photos from Mom and looked at them. Most of the pictures were stock footage seen from tourists; brittle black-and-white Polaroids, fuzzy shots of unknown landmarks printed on thick photo paper with a thin band of white bordering the outer edges. Others were faded color photos of my sister and me gazing at the camera with strained smiles. The newer ones--the pictures taken on Mom's digital camera--were printed in the center of 8X10 white copy paper, the telltale sign of Mom wanting to save a hard copy of the digital image without paying for them to be burned onto a CD. There were friendly, vaguely familiar faces, faces of people I barely remembered, both mingled together with shots of my parents' past that I never knew existed. Scraps of their life thrown together in an unlabeled box. I flipped through my stack of memories, stopping when I spotted one photo that lay hidden at the bottom of the stack, like a hidden snake ready to strike.

It was a 4X5 color picture of a bridge, taken from the inside of a moving car. Beneath the bridge was an endless span of water; a bridge over nothing, going no place. I knew this shot.

"Where was this again?" I asked Mom. She looked at it over my shoulder.

"Oh, some trip your dad and I took a long time ago, probably, but I can't remember. I don't even remember when that was taken."

I stood silently nodding. I remembered. She was right--it was a long time ago. The colors of the photograph were faded now, the edges torn and frayed. The white edges of the snapshot were gray with thumbprints and dust. The last time I saw this photo was when Mom showed it to me one afternoon when I returned to my childhood home to visit them. The year was 1982 and it was summertime. I had moved out the year prior, appearing to all the world like I was a typical idealistic young man who thought he could take the world by storm. In truth, moving out wasn't an act of rebellion as much as an act of avoidance. I hadn't yet told my parents I was gay and I was hoping that by leaving home, I could avoid telling them. Telling people that you're gay was tricky back then, especially when it came to telling your parents. The most hypocritical part of our society is that despite people's claims of "family first", the most important parts of our lives are the parts most people only share with friends.

On this particular visit, I had returned unannounced, assuming I could cop a free dinner. The great thing about being young is that you can always go home for a visit and wind up getting clean laundry, a free meal and--if you're lucky--a free movie. It's like going on a date without the awkwardness of meeting anybody new. When I walked into the house, I caught Mom sitting at the kitchen table smoking a cigarette. She wore an odd grimace and her eyes seemed to gloss over when she saw me, as if something weighed heavily on her mind. She greeted me in a quiet, almost pensive voice and pushed some pictures at me. She sat at the table, narrating through a stack of photos she and Dad had taken on their recent spontaneous road trip. Her voice deteriorated as she spoke, becoming weaker and more breathy, and her speech started to become more like a stutter. She didn't look at me much, instead, she focused on the stack of snapshots spread out on the table. Something was wrong, I could feel it. I thought the clues could be found by looking at the snapshots, but they showed me nothing at all except the usual tourist scenes.

Then I saw a shot of a long vehicle bridge crossing a large expanse of water. I remember thinking how it could be Any Bridge spanning Any Water--like a Beatles song, "Nowhere Bridge sitting in its Nowhere Land." From the angle of the picture, I figured it was taken from the passenger side of the car.

"Where is this?" I asked. Mom shook her head.

"I don't remember." Her voice sounded a million miles away. "I think Florida."

"It looks like the Keys," I urged. "Did you and Dad go to Florida?"

"Oh, I don't remember, exactly. We went all over."

This, I knew, was a lie. Not that they didn't go all over, it was common for them to get into the car and drive into the unknown having no idea where they were going. When they did it, Mom and Dad called it "adventurous". When I did it, it was called "irresponsible". Rather the lie I'm talking about was that Mom didn't remember where the picture was taken. How could she not? Since Dad did all the driving, she must have taken the shot. Besides, how can you not remember going to Florida? We lived outside of Chicago. One doesn't get on the Kennedy Expressway, get lost and suddenly realize you've driven halfway across the country.

Something was definitely wrong.

After a few minutes of silence, she got up and said she was going to get Dad. Several minutes later, she returned to the kitchen alone and sat down at the table again, picking up the pictures and returning them to their box. I was left holding the shot of the bridge. My curiosity piqued, I put the picture back onto the kitchen table and walked down the hallway to their bedroom where I met Dad standing in the doorway. His eyes were narrow slits and his jaw was set so firmly you could see the muscles standing out in his neck. He didn't say hello.

I babbled on about my new job with the ad agency in Chicago, how Mom had shown me pictures of their trip, the weather and just about anything I could think of as I watched him wander to his dresser and paw through the contents of the top drawer. Fearing I had interrupted some fight between the two, I invented some excuse to leave and practically ran out of the house. Later I called my sister and told her what happened.

"They know, Dave," she said simply.

I didn't have to ask anything more. I knew exactly what she meant.

The next day on the phone with Dad, he became very angry, challenging me about "something he heard" about "gay". When my back-pedaling and stammering became so obvious that the conversation deteriorated into long silent pauses, he burst out with, "I don't have a gay son."

"Yes, you do," I replied angrily.

"Then I don't have a son."

I hung up and sat on the hotel bed, stunned and shaken by what had just happened. Shortly thereafter, Mom called to talk with me about the argument with Dad. The conversation ended with her telling me to "give him time and don't call for a while". I did give them time. I didn't call. Neither did they. A little time became almost three years, until the year 1985 when Dad almost died the first time.

So here we were, once again sitting at a kitchen table looking at the same photograph that we looked at twenty years earlier when I lost contact with my parents. On the surface it was a harmless snapshot of a long bridge over sparkling blue water. But to me, that picture represented memories I thought I had forgotten: of feeling that the house I grew up in was no longer my home; of feeling afraid of my own parents; of fearing their disappointed rage was my fault and my responsibility.

I sat frozen to my chair with the picture in my hand. Part of me wanted to tell Mom the story of the first time I saw the picture, but I knew I couldn't. In her face was a far-off longing for the time when she and my father would hop in the car and roam the highways of the rural midwest. When she saw this picture, she didn't remember that time when I visited them in 1982, she remembered being on the road with her husband, discovering the Unknown Bridge for the first time. To her this picture represented a slew of painful memories that stemmed from nostalgia of a dead husband, not fear. I decided not to say anything, choosing instead to return the picture to the stack on the table. Ironic that in 1982 the three of us didn't want to talk to each other. Now, we couldn't because Dad was dead.

***

"Mom, she's flushing me down a toilet."

"It's cute."

"It is not cute," I said for the hundredth time, "she's trying to flush me down a toilet."

"She was five, for God's sake. Get over it."

"We didn't need Doctor Spock. We need Dr. Phil."

When she was sorting out the stacks of family photos, Mom discovered a stack of old family films that she and Dad had transferred to VHS years ago. She thought it would be fun to look at them again. Before I could protest, she had jammed the tape into the machine. I cringed, knowing that I'd have to suffer through hours of old black and white images of people who I barely remembered.

Surprisingly, what came up on the TV was images of myself and my sister when we were children. Tow-haired toddlers running through the living-room carrying stuffed animals and assorted toys, laughing with delight. Then my father was there, about twenty-five, looking young and handsome, picking each of us up in turn and facing the camera, so the lens got a clear shot of our faces.

"That's Dad?" I said astonished. "He had hair?"

"Of course he had hair, you nit-wit," Mom said. "He was so good looking, wasn't he?"

He was. Of course, I couldn't tell my mother that. There is something creepy about thinking your father was sexy.

Suddenly the image changed and my sister and I sat on the sides of the toilet, feet dangling into the bowl splashing each other.

"This is gross, Ma," I said. "We are playing in a toilet."

"We didn't have a lot of money," Mom said, "This was cheap. It's clean water. What's the big deal?"

"It's a toilet."

"So? The dog drinks out of the toilet."

"I know and that's disgusting, too."

"Oh, grow up."

For approximately the next half hour, we sat watching images from the past. My parents didn't appear often in them, at least not together, but when they did, it was obvious that they were enjoying happy times. Mom waving, carefully picking her way through a foot of snow; Dad under the hood of a car, tinkering with the engine; my sister and I chasing each other around a snow covered lawn, pushing each other into the snow.

"You really lived in a basement apartment?"

"We didn't have a lot of money. We had to borrow money so we could get married." I looked at her. "We didn't have a pot to piss in."

"Why didn't you wait?"

"We loved each other," she said simply. "And your dad, being in the service, got housing on base after we got married. It was better than nothing."

"I had no idea."

She nodded and thought about it. "Who would have guessed we could go from two stupid kids who didn't own anything, knowing nothing to owning a house, a car and actually retiring from good jobs? We were so damned young. Neither of us had graduated high school, for God's sake."

"You did good, Ma." She nodded.

I thought about this as I took the videotape out of the player. Maybe this explained why Dad gave me so much grief those times in the past when I wanted to take Mom to New York, or to Europe. It would make sense that, having no education, no money, no investments, virtually nothing except her since he was twenty, he would have seen their relationship as the foundation of his entire life. When I came along, wanting to drag her to parts of the world he felt were dangerous, having no plan, no inkling of how to prepare for an emergency, he probably flipped out. Where I saw adventure and spontaneity, he saw the underpinnings of his world being threatened. No wonder he couldn't stand the idea of taking her overseas. Europe was the unknown. In his world, you didn't go from nothing to something by flirting with the unknown. So this was the key to my over-protective attitude with my mom, and fear of Dad finding out about the sex shop, the red-light district and Mr. No Ass Chap Man: him doubting me was the byproduct of him protecting her. And she, through her travels, enabled him to live vicariously while never losing her own sense of security and, thus, safety.

I yawned and got up. Too much thinking tires me out.

"I'm headed to bed," I said. Mom didn't move. "You going to bed?"

"I think I'll hang out here and watch some TV for awhile."

"Not sleepy?"

"Well," she muttered, "I haven't been sleeping well."

"Want a sleeping pill?" I asked.

She shook her head. "No, I'll just sleep in the recliner."

"Ma, you can not sleep in a recliner."

"Yes, I can. Your father did it all the time. If it's good enough for him, it's good enough for me."

RELATED TANGENT #5
August, 2007

There are two full entries in my journal for the eight days I spent in Tennessee for my father's funeral. One of them recounted a dream I had about my father and me in a bar--which I shared with you earlier. That entry was written in the scrawling, uneven writing of a guy who had just woken from a dream. The other coherent writing was done on the last day of my stay. Everything else written on the pages of my worn journal is chaotic, random notes ranging from words like DAZED to half-finished sentences that in retrospect carry no meaning whatsoever. I often wonder why I didn't use that opportunity to say something interesting or poignant about the experience. My father was dead and I had nothing to say about it.

But the truth is I had much to say about it. I wanted to say how terrifying the experience of losing a parent really is. I wanted to wax philosophical about the dining room chair where Dad used to sit, now remaining empty, as if any visitor who sits in it will be marked for death. I wanted to pour onto the paper every moment of the day, describing in detail about how my body quivered under the grasp of an invisible fist as a giant hand squeezed me, crushing my bones and making breathing impossible. I wanted to record how it feels to walk into the middle of a room, lost in thought, only to jerk yourself awake and realize you're holding your father's shoes in your hand and instead of putting them down, you wonder if you should bring them to the crematorium so someone can put them onto his feet before they burned his body. I wanted to be one of those people who said something important and helpful to people who find themselves facing the death of their parents. But the pages sit blank--a series of random ink doodles are the only entries in my journal the week my father died.

I had to face the fact that there was nothing new I could say to the world. There's nothing new anyone can say to people who have lost a loved one, so trying to do so would just sound trite. What do you say to someone who lost a spouse? I had never been married to someone for forty-six months, much less forty-six years. Relationships are such tenuous things--I learned long ago never to ask why someone loves their partner. They don't know. When it comes to love, most people eventually do what their hearts tell them to do. Reason has nothing to do with it. Logic is thrown out the window with the first utterance of "I love you". Both parties settle into a comfortable and familiar pattern that becomes this thing called "relationship" until they die or something thumps their petrie dish life. What could I possibly write that would do justice to the years of "What do you think?", "We bought a house" or "I never said that!"?

I wrote, instead, about the final year of graduate school, when I found myself hanging out with my parents more than ever before. "I drive your father crazy," Mom said to me during one of my many visits.

"It's good to know, Mom," I assured her. "When he's hauled away by the men in the funny white coats, I'll know who to blame."

"Shut up," she said, typing into the computer. "These are the financial records." The printer chugged to life, spit out a sheet of paper lined with numbered columns and Mom thrust it at me. "This is the column for the check number, this is the name of the company and the date the check cleared." She snatched it back and filed it. "Then I have a record of when I paid what."

"Mom, that's what online banking is for." She looked at me oddly. "You don't have to print it. You can call up the history of your checking account whenever you want and look at it. God made servers so you don't have to keep paper copies of shit."

"Well, I just do it anyway. Just in case." I didn't ask "just in case what?" like I wanted to ask. I suppose the possibility of nuclear attack always looms over us. Although if that were to happen, I doubt if a mushroom cloud will ask to see printouts of your financial records.

I mentioned to my father how Mom's addiction to creating useless paperwork was reaching critical levels and asked him if it was time for an intervention. He didn't seem too interested in discussing the waste of paper, nor the possibility of psychiatric help. I think I woke him from a nap, as his voice was thick and heavy with sleep as he said, "Yeah, I know. It makes her happy."

"Dad--she's in there making pie charts of paid bills."

"Who cares? It keeps her busy." Then he fell asleep. I wanted to change the channel on the TV, but the remote lay in his lap. There was no way I was reaching for it.

One of Mom's compulsions is, as she puts it, "tidying up". As I see it, she doesn't clean a house; she beats it into submission. Constant dishwashing, vacuuming, dusting and spot checks keep her whirling like a tornado in Kansas for hours on end. Dad never complained, though, nor did the rest of the family. As long as we were willing to put up with the vacuum as background music to the nightly news, none of us had to get our hands dirty. Dad found it particularly advantageous. In exchange for an OCD housekeeper, all he had to do was listen to Mom chattering away about the unfolding events of the day and let her shoot random questions at him while he watched The Price is Right. *She wasn't interested in the answers. She was interested in knowing he was there.*

The whole week I was visiting them, I found myself remembering these events and wondered what Mom would do when she didn't hear the answers anymore. What happens when, in the middle of vacuuming the couch, she shouts out, "What do you want for lunch?" and silence is the only answer? I'm used to this, because I live with a cat. Anyone who lives with a cat will tell you they are terrible conversationalists.

***

It's frustrating: In this world of *Car Repair for Dummies* and *Dating for Dummies* and *PCs for Dummies*, and everyone from the local church to the local hospital wants to give you "helpful handouts" and "easy acronyms to remember", there is no easy-to-read *How To* book for burying a dead parent. There needs to be a checklist for the family of the dearly departed; a guide that tells you to get several signed copies of a death certificate, how to request the bank remove a name from the checkbook, how to tell the car repair place that the point of contact is no longer living, and how to tell well-meaning friends not to say, "Oh, I'm sorry" one more time or you'll shoot them.

I've noticed the most helpful things in the world are rarely easy to obtain.

So looking back on the incident, I know why there are no entries in my journal that week, but only ink doodles. Entries are for remembering bits of your life. Blank pages are for forgetting them.

JOURNAL ENTRY
AUGUST 6, 2007

Last night, Sunday, August 5.

Mom and I prepared to go to bed about midnight. I had already changed into my shorts and T-shirt which I slept in while visiting at my parents' and she hadn't changed out of her shorts which she had used all day. She hugged me tightly, as if fearing I would disappear.

"I'm glad you're here," she said. I nodded and murmured something I don't remember. "Your dad always said that if something happened you'd be here."

"Of course I would," I said. How do you respond to that?

She hugged me tighter. "I am so proud of you—we both were."

"I don't know why," I said because it's the truth.

"Are you kidding?" she said in my ear. "Lots of reasons. One time your dad watched you interpreting on stage and he said, 'You know—he's pretty good'. You turned out great. Both you and your sister did. Your dad and I did okay."

I think we all want to hear things like that from our parents. Despite the fact that we all grow up, leave home, pursue fucked-up lives of our own, there's nothing that can substitute for kudos from a parent. I've spent years of therapy time and hundreds of dollars trying to NOT feel that I needed to hear those words but it hadn't helped. Ironic that now one of them is gone and I don't need to hear the words as desperately, is when I hear them.

Fast Forward to: Seattle, 2009
Two years after Dad's death

"This is my favorite place!" Mom giggled as she unhooked her arm from mine and trotted towards the store's entrance, nearly knocking over an elderly couple in the process. Great.This makes the fifth or sixth favorite "favorite" store this afternoon. I watch her plow through the herd of high school students standing in a circle in front of the entrance, cell phones in hand, oblivious to the world, and hear Mom's terse, "Excuse me", as they toppled against each other like a gaggle of Gap mannequins floating on the open sea. By the time they were able to rip their attention away from the electronic leashes and look up, Mom had already made it over the threshold of the store and into the den of bright lights, colorful signs and advertising lies that I knew exhausted but also thrilled her. Mom's an addict, strung out on the tasty oblivion of consumerism which she mainlines through a Visa card.

The sign above the entrance read BROOKSTONE.

Brookstone. Where have I heard that name before? I let the name seep into my brain like spilt coffee on my freshly laundered and pressed pants. It sounded so familiar. It must be some kind of chain store, or one that advertises widely, as I don't shop, unless said shopping is done under extreme duress, such as clutching a gift certificate in my hand, or dragged to the Ross-For-Less store by a well-meaning friend who has a gun pointed at my head. I was born with a DNA defect that causes me to break out in hives whenever I get near a mall. The malady is compounded by the insanity of the capitalistic mass marketing techniques. The sheer number of choices numbs my mind. Stores don't sell just pants, but the same pants in different colors. Usually, I wander around a store until I throw my arms in the air and run away, screaming like a little girl, or crawl into a corner and howl, "JUST TELL ME WHICH PANTS TO BUY!" Seriously . . . how many choices do people need? There is a fine line between consumer choice and just-buy-the-damn-things-already. Signs are everywhere, screaming: BUY NOW! SAVE OVER 20%! Why don't we buy nothing and save 100%? How about signs in windows that preach the truth: COME IN! BUY STUFF YOU DON'T REALLY NEED ON A CHARGE CARD THAT GOUGES YOU FOR INTEREST! BRING IT HOME, WEAR IT ONCE, THEN FORGET ABOUT IT!

For years, I've thrived on Value Village, Goodwill and the kindness of strangers for my clothing, which has culminated in a line of fashion that runs the gambit from green checked flannel to red striped flannel. Lately, however, I've discovered the creme de la creme of thrift stores: Jewish Women's Auxiliary. In graduate school,

I found a morning suit for $25.00, a tuxedo for $60 and a wide assortment of jackets, shirts and shoes for pennies on the dollar. We're not talking the cheap wingtips with soles worn through that a stodgy banker threw in for a tax deduction. We're talking clothes given-to-old-Jews-who-died-before-they-had-a-chance-to-wear-them kind of clothing--with tags still attached and everything. I'm not sure if I have a low standard of dress, if Jews have a higher standard of dress, both or neither. All I know is that show me a Jewish Women's Auxiliary and I'll show you one happy homo with checkbook in hand.

Due to my acquisition-retardation condition, my familiarity with store names is limited, which is how I knew Brookstone must be a chain or advertised widely enough to be seen by me--a guy who doesn't own a television. The name hung around the back of my mind as I motioned the elderly couple past me, circled the high schoolers still fixated on their cell phones and into the store in pursuit of Mom.

I found her a few feet to my left, behind a stack of colorful boxes and below a huge banner announcing ANNUAL SALE! DISCOUNTS OF UP TO 25%. The banner was caked with dust.

The woman bobbing her head at Mom had a thin face, huge eyes and a mouth that looked too big to fit onto any human. Her hair was teased so violently the follicles were still in therapy for an inferiority complex. It loomed over her, like a Zeppelin preparing for take off. Behind her stood a young man wearing a brown smock, horn-rimmed glasses and an identical broad smile. All-in-all, they looked like living bookends of a Marketing and Design Department gone postal. As I approached Mom, hoping to grab her arm before she reached for her wallet, the smell of the sales people assaulted me. The woman emanated a combination of tangy scents and flowery essences. The young man smelled like Old Spice. My father wore Old Spice. My dad and every other middle-aged dad in town. It was the official scent of midwestern Dads in 1960. Was it possible I have reached that age when outdated colognes are in fashion again? I plunged between them, who, together amounted to an olfactory equivalent of the *Peanuts* character Pigpen, and hovered near Mom's side. Why is it people complain about second-hand cigarette smoke, but it's still legal to asphyxiate people with perfume?

"Your father and I used to come into this place all the time," she said, fondling a battery powered toy helicopter. "Your father would sit in the massage chair and I'd play with the toys. We had so much fun!"

Her eyes lit on something else deep inside of the store and she disappeared behind a pyramid of cardboard boxes.

Damn. She's using again. We've found the neighborhood pusher. Its name is BROOKSTONE.

"Good morning," the smiling young woman with Therapy Hair crooned, pegging Mom for the addict that she is. "Want to watch movies widescreen on your iPod!" It wasn't a question. It was a command.

Mom stumbled towards her, all glassy eyed and drooling, high on the possibility of whipping out the charge card. "What's that?"

"A wonderful new companion for your iPod," she said cheerily. Her face didn't move, but parts of her eyebrow cracked. "You put your iPod or iPhone into this device," she demonstrated by placing her own iPhone between two speakers approximately five inches square. "Then, when you turn the iPod onto its side, LIKE MAGIC! You can watch your rented movies on the wide screen!" Her voice slid the scale from excited to orgasmic. I feared she would faint.

Mom watched the young woman grab the prop iPod and twist it onto its side. The iPod moved a couple inches, then jammed halfway between the two speakers.

"I'm new," she explained, her smile never fading. "It turned earlier." She swiveled the iPod upright, then attempted to spin it onto its side again. This time it slid easily between the two speakers. The entire system was about a foot long by five inches high.

"It's perfect for viewing on a plane. Do you travel?" Her eyes sought me out.

DON'T LOOK INTO HER EYES! I told myself. I always found it best to treat salespeople like vampires and avoid direct contact. Too late. Her gaze caught mine and the tracker beam of consumerism tugged at my brain. I felt the pressure to respond. "Not as much as I'd like--"

"I understand," she said with a voice so soft I could nap on it. "It's hard to sit in one place for those long, long, hours, isn't it?"

"Totally," I agreed.

"Well, then you can put this on your lap, plug in the iPod and watch a film!" Her smile returned, she jumped in her seat and winked. She seemed so friendly. Honest. Understanding. Maybe I judged her too harshly. Maybe she wasn't a vixen hunting a sale. Maybe she really cared about airplane-numb-ass. "You do have an iPod, don't you?"

I nodded.

"I thought so. Everyone does these days." She laughed and I laughed with her. Her laughter resounded like little bells. She winked again. I felt warm. Was the air conditioner working?

"The batteries go in here," she continued, flipping the system onto its front and showing me the back of the device. "They last long enough for an entire movie."

"That is so cool, David!" Mom said, appearing at my side. When did she get back?

"Well . . ." I stammered. "What about the iPod? Doesn't this drain the battery of the iPod?"

She leaned over and picked up a smaller box. "This is a replacement battery!" Her exuberance was infectious. I found myself giggling. She slipped the sleek metal contraption out of its comfy cardboard home and held it out to me between two manicured fingers. "When the iPod's battery dies, you just pop this into the bottom and like magic, you've got a fully recharged battery again!"

I had to admit, it sounded really cool. Far too often I've gotten on the plane only to discover I left my book in the suitcase, or at home, and tried to amuse myself by reading the in-flight magazine. That's it! The in-flight magazine! Brookstone has advertised in the shopping magazine stuck in the seat pocket in front of me! I looked around the store and realized Mom had led me to the Promised Land of gadgets: the noiseless standup fan that deionized the air; the digital photo frame; the Pico Pocket Projector; the Grill Alert Talking Remote Meat Thermometer; the Anti-Snore Pillow! I love this store!

"So I need to get the portable speakers and the battery charger?" I asked.

"Right," she said. "With those two, you can have over four hours of movie-watching." She touched my arm and the enthusiasm infused me. I felt my heart quicken and my breath catch. I must have four hours of movie-watching. I will die without four hours of movie-watching.

I did a quick calculation. The portable iPod travel speakers were only $49.99 and the portable, rechargeable replacement battery was on sale for $29.99. Seventy dollars is such a small price to pay for four hours of in-flight entertainment.

"Do you sell the movies?"

"You can download them directly from iTunes! Isn't that simple!"

"I've never done that before," I sighed, a heaviness returning to my chest. I knew this was too good to be true.

"It's soooooo easy," she crooned, patting me on the arm. "The movies rent for $1.99. Then you have thirty days to view them."

"Only a buck ninety-nine?" I felt lighter. Maybe there was relief for my in-flight boredom.

"Do you have earphones? If not, we sell them over there." She pointed to the back of the store.

$49.99 for the speakers, $29.99 for the rechargeable replacement battery and $1.99 for a movie. That's affordable. I turned to ask Mom what she thought, but she was in the far corner of the store, standing next to another young man in a brown smock at a table with miniature frogs inside a miniature, plastic aquarium, under a sign that read, OWN YOUR OWN ECO-SYSTEM.

"Just a second," I said to the woman, "I need to ask my Mom."

"These are so cruel," Mom said as I plodded up behind her. "Look at this. This aquarium can't be more than eight inches square and these poor frogs have to live inside. That's just mean."

"Well," the deep voiced, smooth skinned salesman said, "the entire aquarium is a miniature eco-system. It remains in perfect harmony." He lifted one of the tiny aquariums.

"The plants provide oxygen, the algae grows on the stem, which feeds the frogs and the bacteria will take care of the frog's waste products. When you think about it, it is the way nature meant it to be. We've only brought Mother Nature back into balance."

I nodded. I couldn't agree more. Before humans came along with Tupperware, plastic shopping bags and silicone, everything was biodegradable. A hundred years ago, the cycle was complete. Now, we have garbage barges floating alongside New York waiting for a place to decompose.

"You can have your very own little world--a PLANET if you think about it. And it's on sale," he smiled. He looked so . . . innocent . . . honest . . . friendly. "You can save $20.00 if you buy it today."

"Really?" I asked. I did some quick math in my head: if I bought the frogs today and saved twenty bucks, with the money I saved, I could buy the rechargeable replacement battery for the iPod wide screen movie watcher. That way I could do my part to save the environment while simultaneously avoiding boredom on my flights.

I nudged Mom, but I hit only empty air.

"Just a second," I said. "I need to talk to my Mom."

I found her standing by the U-control Silver Bullet mini-RC helicopters.

"Look at these!"

From nose to tail, they measured about four inches, and, like advertised, FIT EASILY IN THE PALM OF YOUR HAND! While not perfect replicas of real helicopters, they looked pretty snappy, like some futuristic built-by-Q-specifically-for-James Bond contraption. They came in two colors and radiated "cool": neon red and cobalt blue. Cobalt blue is my favorite shade. When I was a kid I would ask Santa that all my toys come painted in cobalt blue. They didn't, of course, so I deemed Santa either mean or color-blind, depending on my age and what other cool things he got me.

"They are radio-controlled by a control box like this," a young, smooth-skinned man in a brown smock said, showing us the square device that looked like a video game controller. He looked so . . . innocent . . . honest . . . friendly. "Watch this."

He pushed one of the two buttons on the contraption and the helicopter ascended in a flurry of blades. With a nudge of the second button, the helicopter dived to the left and then to the right. Within minutes, the tiny dive bomber was dodging in and out of the display racks.

"That is so cool!" Mom grinned. "I love this store!"

"Want to try it?" the man asked Mom.

She snatched the control box and held it in front of her. "Like this?" she asked and pushed a button. The fiery red helicopter flew up and crashed against a light fixture. It fell like a rock, landing at our feet.

"Oh, well," Mom sighed, "another one bites the dust." She handed the control box to the young man.

"Here, I'll show you," the young man said. He picked up the toy and placed it onto a stack of boxes displaying pictures of the toy helicopters. He pressed the remote control box into my hand. "Press this lever just hard enough to raise the helicopter into the air."

"They're indestructible?" I asked.

"Pretty much, yes. The parts are flexible plastic, not rigid. That provides for plenty of crashes."

Mom watched as he demonstrated. Once the helicopter was safely on the ground again, she snatched the controller from me.

"Hey!" I tugged back. "You had a chance!"

"This is not going to get the best of me!"

"There's another one over there!"

"Here, I'll get you both one," the salesman said, thrusting another controller into my hand.

Mom pushed the button on her control box. The helicopter veered towards the chipper young woman with the Zeppelin hair and slammed into her butt. She jumped back in surprise. Her hair did not move.

"Oh! I'm so sorry!" Mom said.

"It's okay. I love those toys," she laughed and handed Mom the helicopter. Then she turned her sunny disposition on me. "They're only $29.99 apiece or two for $49.99."

"Rechargeable?" I asked.

"You can buy the rechargeable batteries near the check out." She smiled. "They're on sale. Two for one."

I did the quick math in my head. If I bypassed the eco-friendly frogs, ditched the iPod wide screen movie player and went with the helicopter, I not only provided myself with hours of amusement, but could provide hours of amusement for my boyfriend as well. I saw us sitting in his living room, he with a glass of wine, me with the phone pressed to my ear, dive-bombing my annoying cat. Finally! A way for me to strike back against her piercing scream for attention.

I must have these helicopters. I will die without these helicopters.

"Your mom's over there," the man said.

I found her with a solar-powered flashlight with a hand crank. "The crank is for the times when there is no sun. You just crank this and WHAM! You're never in the dark again."

"How much?" I asked.

"Only $9.99," the young man said. "It's on sale."

"Well, that wasn't bad," Mom said as we hustled out of Brookstone, bags in hand. "Under an hour. Your father and I could stay in that store for hours."

"Really," I said. "It's a huge toy shop for adults."

"No, that place in New York was a toy shop for adults. This is just fun."

"I'm telling you, Mom, Americans spend too much on disposable crap. We need to start picking up a book."

"Nice helicopters." She muttered, rolling her eyes.

"This is different! I never buy fun stuff."

"It is fun stuff, isn't it?" she asked, taking my hand. "Your dad said the same thing. He loved that store."

"Yeah, I can understand why. I love it, too."

"Well," she said, patting my hand. "We all need a little fun in our lives."

"Yeah, I guess so." I said to empty air. She had wandered off into Tiffany's.

EPILOGUE

"I've decided I'm moving."

"No shit?"

"I need to get away. This is the house I had with your father and I just don't want to stay here anymore."

I smiled to myself. It was an act I knew she would do, which was why I asked her to wait a year after Dad died. The best advice I ever heard coming from someone is that once your partner dies, you never want to make life-changing decisions the first year. Luckily, Mom had done what I asked and stayed put. Over a year had passed and it was now in her hands.

"I have to make a life for myself," she said. "I need to move on."

"I'm proud of you, Ma," I said. "I think it's a great decision. Where you going?"

"I was thinking Florida." She paused.

I paused. I've always hated Florida. The weather is as humid as the midwest and hot as the south without the charm of either.

"I really don't want you moving to Florida."

"Why?"

"It's gross. And it's so . . . weird. Like California with alligators."

"Well, where do you think I should look at?"

I paused for a moment, knowing that I should tell her what I had been thinking for months. I thought about the ride home from the airport, over a year ago, when she rambled on about inane and unrelated things and feeling so angry at her that she wasn't more upset that Dad was dead. I felt ashamed of myself and ashamed of the way I thought of her that night; for while the confusion and anger over her illogical attitude consumed me, I had a job to return to after the funeral. I had bills to pay, a car to wash, a kitchen to clean. Mom had all those things, too, of course, but I was used to doing these things alone. She was used to shooting Dad random questions while he watched *The Price is Right*.

I mentally flipped through the freeze frames of time in my mind's eye, replaying all the "You need to go to summer recreation" or "Get a job! Life isn't easy, you know!" or "Nothing's free!" and remembered how mystified I was that someone who was supposed to love their kids could be so harsh to them, forcing them to do things they didn't want to do. I saw myself as a kid, a teenager and then older, listening to her reprimand me for lapses in judgement, using the same voice as she used now: Calm. Cool. Collected.

Then the pictures in my mind fluttered to a stop on an image from several months previous. We were in a car for this argument, naturally, as driving is a surefire way to ignite a total mental meltdown with me. I abhor being in a car. The only thing worse than being in a car is being in the unfortunate position of having to drive one. Usually, Mom is more than happy to leap behind the wheel of the Buick and play the role of chauffeur, as long as I'm willing to pay the price--usually a nice bottle of red wine, preferably by a local winery. The only problem arises when she isn't driving; this means I'm driving. Me + road + driving = textbook road rage.

So in this memory, I'm the one who is driving. Mom's in the passenger seat asking about my new job which isn't going well. At one point she sighs and says, "I just want you to be happy."

That was the last straw. This constant discussion about my irritating job, combined with the unexpectedly cold weather in Seattle and the fact that everyone on the road that day was not competent to drive a skateboard, much less an automobile, made me snap. I shot back, "Don't give me that. If you want to disagree, just say so. But don't spew trivial blah-blah. It's insulting."

She didn't miss a beat with her reply. "You don't understand, because you're not a mother. One of the things that makes a mother truly happy is knowing her children are safe and content."

"So just because people are safe and content, mothers everywhere leap up and down in relief and joy."

"Yes, they do," Mom said. Then, after a long pause, "And stop being a sarcastic shit. You have no idea what it's like being a mother. When you do, you can talk about it."

Being a mother? Is she kidding me? I've always viewed a pregnancy as nothing more than a 9-month battle against a parasite. (Stop crinkling your nose and think about it: The unborn fetus will take what it can from the host body to survive. In fact, the fetus will often inflict great damage ranging from swollen feet to a shrinking bladder to strange urges for pickles at 3 AM.) and the act of giving birth a prolonged torture. So how in the hell is your children's happiness suddenly paramount in your life?

I thought about all these random thoughts while she waited for me to share my feelings on her moving. It struck me that maybe there was something to that "mother" comment. Maybe all those years of watching my sister and me fall off bikes, stub our toes, date some really horrible people and put the white underwear in with the red shirts were harder on my parents than I suspected. Maybe those acts of adolescent defiance my sister and I inflicted upon Mom did more than allow us to act out our frustration and stubbornness. Maybe they forced her into a position of making a choice about her life too. Was she going to be an overprotective enabler who will teach her kids to believe that they will always be rescued after making a stupid decision, or was she going to create members of society who will be able to accept failure and disappointment and face the consequences of their actions? Maybe her distant, seemingly uninterested attitude toward us when we were young was a role she felt she had to play in order to raise two children in an ever-changing, ever-more-complex world. She could look unaffected and unemotional when, inside, she was crumbling, or worse, wanting to throttle her kids for being such dopes.

In my family, self-actualization and enlightenment are stumbled upon; usually during car rides, over food, or while talking about something else.

I thought about telling her that over the last year and a half, I've spent a lot of time chatting with the mothers I know and I finally got it: Mom had learned the art of acting earlier than I. Mothers of her generation are like stage actors. Just like their scenery-chomping counterparts, mothers go for the jugular in an attempt to reach their objective; namely, you learning what you need to learn. Mothers of her generation didn't mutate into demanding, chore-enforcing demons for no reason. Mothers of her generation didn't want to be your friend, didn't want to process their kids feelings and--when you swore in public--slapped you across the mouth. Mothers of her generation are like most other mammals--they want to help their offspring reach adulthood without getting eaten by predators. They thought putting on a "Mom Face" would protect their young by toughening them up; get them to understand the world isn't fair; help prepare them for the world. They knew the price of raising a kid, and they were willing to pay the cost. Even if that cost was themselves.

Maybe that's the role she was playing that day a year ago in the car as we drove home from the Nashville airport after Dad died; that night she seemed so calm, cool and collected, while I sat in the backseat wondering what the hell was going on. Maybe that night she was falling back into the familiar petrie dish, refusing to jump no matter how hard her world had been thumped. She was hunkering down, saying, "Ha! I smite thee down, facts! I will believe what I choose to believe, despite all logic to the contrary, for I am comfortable in my petrie dish!" the way so many of my friends defend their abusive, alcoholic, unemployed partners--familiarity is better than loneliness.

Regardless of why mothers do what they do, their children have no idea how deep the act of impartial observer hurts. Perhaps all children will never know when an act of pretending to not be emotionally affected by your children stops and the act of healing starts. Perhaps it's for the best.

Perhaps I'm wrong; I have no kids, only a cat--and she doesn't care about much of anything one way or the other. Except catnip. Never skimp on the catnip.

In a flash, I found myself worrying less about my pain and more about Mom's.

"I think you should consider Seattle." I finally said.

"With you?"

"Why not?"

"Well," she thought for a minute. "I guess we've survived worse."

"Yeah, Ma, we have," I agreed. "So when are you moving?"

THE END

Kathy + Robert,

Thank you so
much for everything

David Alan

De, 2013

Made in the USA
Charleston, SC
08 November 2013